Praise for *Unsexed*

"From its opening pages, we know *Unsexed* is going to offer us vulnerability and wisdom mixed with tragedy, which is a particular kind of unflinching honesty: one that has set aside fear in favor of truth. In this raw and gritty memoir, DelVecchio reveals what it means to be a daughter longing for nourishment, a lover wanting to be respected, and a mother who has unwittingly learned exactly how to love. She never claims to have come out on the other side all shiny and happy, only renewed. Sometimes another person's story reminds us of the will and strength we all have running deep inside—*Unsexed* is one of those stories."

—Shuly Xóchitl Cawood, author of the memoir
The Going and Goodbye

"*Unsexed* is a searingly honest, painful, beautifully expressed and ultimately transcendent story about the damage caused by the absence of love, and the healing that becomes possible with truth and courage."

—Adrienne Moore, author of *Seven Tears in the Sea*

"*Unsexed* is an amazingly honest memoir that's hard to put down. DelVecchio's ability to render her story with no exaggerations or evasions makes it a page-turning book. The author doesn't attempt to hide the damage to her own psyche caused by these experiences, and readers will find themselves rooting for her as the book reaches its end. Highly recommended for book clubs, who will find a great deal to discuss."

—Gabi Coatsworth, author of *Love's Journey Home* and
A Beginner's Guide to Starting Over

UNSEXED

Unsexed

*Memoirs of a
Prostitute's Daughter*

Marina DelVecchio, PhD

SHE WRITES PRESS

Published 2024
Printed in the United States of America
Print ISBN: 978-1-64742-694-1
E-ISBN: 978-1-64742-695-8
Library of Congress Control Number: 2024905755

For information, address:
She Writes Press
1569 Solano Ave #546
Berkeley, CA 94707

Interior design by Stacey Aaronson

She Writes Press is a division of SparkPoint Studio, LLC.

Names and identifying characteristics have been changed to protect the privacy of certain individuals.

"Come you spirits that tend on mortal thoughts, unsex me here and fill me here, and fill me from the crown to the toe, top-full of direst cruelty! Make thick my blood."

—Lady Macbeth

"Censor the body and you censor breath and speech at the same time. Write yourself. Your body must be heard."

—Helene Cixous, "The Laugh of the Medusa"

PROLOGUE:
(LOVE) LETTER TO MY
ESTRANGED BODY

I haven't always loved you. You're like a child I was forced to give birth to and raise against my will. One I could never abort, given to me by force, through rape and abuse and obligation. I couldn't give you away, place you in a basket, cover you up with blankets, and leave you for someone else to care for—at a hospital, a fire department, a police station. So I have carried you like a bag filled with jagged rocks upon my back, unable to put you down or abandon you.

You go where I go, a bad memory I can't dip into a bottle of whiteout to erase from my existence. I have raised you without choice or consent. You are mine and mine alone. A stranger I pretend to know and live with because I cannot kill you, stifle you, make you disappear. You are there all the time, reminding me of trauma I cannot ignore, like an ugly, red, glaring scar that runs from my chin down to my vaginal opening, hiding beneath the carefully chosen clothes I pull over your arms and legs to make you appear normal and palatable to onlookers.

It is because of you that my bones shrink when my children touch my toes, my elbows, my kneecaps, when I disappear into the black folds of darkness when one of them accidentally hits me in the face, or hugs me for too long, the infrahyoid muscles tensing beneath my neck skin, my clavicle pushing against my flesh, vibrating with anxiety, for one moment of relief. It's because of you I did not have sex for ten years, lying beside my husband each night with a wall so heavy, so fortified with shame and neglect, that it would take years just to dismantle it.

Because of you, I walk the quiet and lonely lengths of my life with fear as my constant companion, a shadowy lover who owns me with force, securing manacles about my throat and ankles and wrists, binding me to him out of terror. You're the reason I can't sit beside my mother in her hospital bed without going into convulsions when she inches her body toward my own, clasping her hand in mine. You curl me into you, against my will, when I am touched by her, by my husband, by anyone. But you don't explain to me the reasons behind your resistance to touch, to physical expressions of love, leaving me alone in my inarticulateness, searching for words that are kind and can explain to the loves of my life why I shrink from them. Why intimacy makes every bone in my body throb with irritation, cracking and bending under the weight of what feels like an anvil pressing down on my lungs, squeezing all the air out of them until all that's left is a flat mass of matter, fractured and worn out.

There is no peace with you, no reprieve, no pause. No comfort. No love. Just pain followed by more pain that makes me teeter like a toddler off-balance on the precarious balance beam of life constructed out of brokenness, because you never let me go, never let me rest. You slow me down, force me to stay in one place when all I want is to run, to disappear, to die. Yes, to die sometimes. But you won't let me. You keep me around against my will. You have a mind of your own, and I resent you for it.

It's been hard to care for you and even more difficult to love you. You're draining, sucking the remaining drops of energy I have through my pores, a painfully tedious process that never ends.

I should love you. I should care for you in the way I care for the bodies of my two children. After all, I wouldn't have been able to push them into this life without you, without your strength, your immense tolerance for pain. I know I should worship you and think of you as belonging to me, advocating for me, but I often want to mute you, to wish you away.

I have even tried killing you. More than once. If it weren't for my kids, you and I wouldn't own a space in this life. I stay for them. That kind of loss would change them, make them as dark and as cavernous as I am, trapped inside your shell. If it weren't for them, I'd have done away with both of us a long time ago.

Since I can't seem to find the power to kill you off like a villainous character in a book, I am now trying to know you, not as I was taught to see you, as the bastard I never wanted to raise, but as you are. As you want me to see you. As you want to be known.

In the same ways that I have wanted to be known by my mothers. Athanasia, my birth mother, who taught me that women's bodies could be served to men for a price and who taught me to fear your desires. And Ann, the second one, who adopted me without knowing me, without loving me, rejecting the experiences that brought me to her, damaged and starving for everything she would deny me. She taught me self-loathing and self-control. How to turn off warmth and deny myself love.

Neither mother saw me, birthing in me a hunger to be seen, to be loved.

But today, I stand before this mirror, bare and vulnerable, hoping that through my uncovering, I will locate the reasons for my misgivings, my punishments, my refusals of you as you desperately hold onto the hem of my pants like an orphan cling-ing to the only person assigned to you as your mother. It is the same way my two mothers refused me, modeling my treatment of you.

Our story then, yours and mine, begins with our mothers, their relationship to their bodies and their relationship to you and me. It is perhaps the origin of our relationship, a union of forced endurance I am still trying to unravel and understand to love you.

And in the end, I suppose, to love myself.

PART I

Athanasia, The Whore-Mother

WHORING FOR CHICKEN

I don't remember the first time I had sex.

But I do remember the first time my mother, Athanasia, had sex for money. For food, really. A sumptuous scented, piping hot, roasted chicken doused with Greek herbs that made my mouth water and my stomach grumble with longing.

I was four, and it was during the summer of 1975, in the poor, abandoned construction sites of Peristeri in Greece. This is one of my earliest and most profound memories, cocooned with protective gear and locked in the back of my memory box, where I keep all the early recollections of my childhood.

Crowded and bumping against each other, they are all fragmented images, riddled with blood and violence and sex and childhood neglect, and I had to paste them together the way one attaches puzzle pieces they found in the attic from a childhood long past. Some images are missing, while others are tattered, with ripped-off corners that don't seem to fit anywhere. Even the cover of the box that housed them is gone, missing the visual model needed to see what all the pieces, when put together, would look like. Loose and scattered, I laid them all out on the table and reconstructed where they belonged, the pattern often dependent on a rough estimate of my age.

Homeless at the time, I recall the night my mother walked into the building we found refuge in, still under construction and abandoned by the crew during the evenings. Her words reached for me like thick ivy, unruly and knotted, rolling and coiling their way from her lips to my ears, wrapping around me with smooth precision, sucking the air out of my lungs.

"I did it," she told Kristos, her pimp. Her lover. The man she would spend the next thirty years of her life with. She didn't look at him, or me, as she tossed the bag of food at his feet.

The tantalizing scents of broiled chicken invaded my nostrils with force, promising to fill the hungry, lonely, caved in spaces of my stomach with sustenance. With relief. My limbs jerked with want, but I forced them to be still, like stones set on the cold, hard, unfinished floor of the building. The smell of a cooked meal moved me, tantalized me, but I was unwilling to show weakness to the two adults I loathed.

My mother. Her pimp.

The two people I had to rely on for my survival. To show them I wanted—needed—something they could provide was dangerous. What would they want in return? What more would they take from me?

"I did it," were the only words she said. At least, the only words I remember her saying. The only words that stayed with me, reminding me not to forget where I came from. What she was. How dangerous she was to trust and love. Words that came out in a clipped tone surrendered to the stony and rigid spaces of the building that would shelter us for the night.

I knew what my mother meant with those words. She traded her body for our dinner. Until then, I hadn't known men would give up meals for sex. That sex was a commodity with that kind of value. Sex for money, yes. I had seen it, been around it. But food for sex and sex for food? That was a first.

I may have been small and young, but sex was not a new phenomenon for me. My mother had sex with men while my father, John, was out at work collecting trash and depositing it into the truck as it rolled from one city corner to the next in our neighborhood.

One man, in particular, passed by my small body on the steps leading to our home. When we had a home. Before my father left us. This man was a recurring fixture, parking his motorcycle and bouncing up the stairs that led to the home we all shared with my mother. Stavros, my older brother by a year, called him "the fisherman," because the stink of fish emanated from his pores, forcing our noses to scrunch up against our unwashed faces. Sometimes, he brought us ice cream, and my brother and I licked the milky sweet substance as if it were the only thing we had eaten that day. Probably because it was.

Our mother met him at the door, smiling, her arms pulling him to her, their bodies crashing, hips grinding. Our ears listened to the sighs and sounds of their sex. The laughter that followed their lovemaking. Their sex was fun and light, and Stavros and I, witnesses to our mother's infidelity, looked at each other with discomfort and then looked away. We were complicit. He took our mother into his arms while we ate the ice cream he gave us. We licked it until it was all gone, disappearing into the grumbling caverns of our stomachs where our guilt and collusion lay in wait, ready to strike with accusatory whines.

This was before my father left us to move in with his sister. Before Kristos took his place as father and protector. Corruptor. The man who reminded me of my place as a girl, encumbered and unprotected.

The sex that Kristos and my mother had was not fun. Not light at all. They had sex in front of me, while I pretended to sleep a few inches from them, my small body embracing the tiny bundle of my baby sister, Eleni, to keep us warm, her cooing barely drowning out the grunts and moans of their coupling.

Their sex was wild, hard, without the laughter I once encountered between her and her lover, the fish-smelling motorcycle

man. It was a struggle, a battle for possession. They each smoked
a cigarette afterward. They lay on the blanket, naked, uncon-
cerned with concealing their privates or the stench of their antics,
filling me with loathing, nausea rising to my throat. I remember
the way my bones went rigid, too, and how I took deep breaths
to loosen them.

It hurt when my limbs clenched like that, like some sort of
vice kept them still and motionless, cutting off the blood from
circulating to the rest of my organs needing warmth. Like my
fingers, growing cold and painfully straight so I couldn't even curl
them into fists to pound against his chest or her grinning mouth.

I wanted to run, to look away, but my body wouldn't move.
It froze in place, in time, like an icicle waiting to melt away by
natural means, with no volition in sight. I had no control over
what happened to me. Over what happened to my body. I only
had control over what I ate and from whom I would take food.
This collusion of food and sex has changed me. The association
between sex and food, sex and need, sex and desire became this
enmeshed knot of roots and vines that still thrives in the pit of my
stomach and burns my own sex.

So fearful am I—still—of using my sex for trade that I have
become meticulous about when I have sex and with whom. In
fact, I married the first man I had sex with, and it took me a year
and a half to trust him enough to go all the way. Twelve years
into our marriage, when I no longer felt safe to love him, to be
loved by him, I refused to have sex with him. To do so, to have
sex without love, would mark me with my first experiences with
sex—my mother and her lovers, my mother and her pimp, my
mother and her johns.

I was unsexed. For ten years in my marriage, I was in control. I was safe.

ॐ

"One thing about whoring: It put a chicken on the table," is a line that grabbed me by the throat while reading Jeannette Walls's memoir *The Glass Castle*. She was a hungry child, her parents nomadic and unstable creatures who couldn't keep their jobs, stay sober, or raise their three children with enough food on the table or security in their lives to sustain them.

This line comes from a time when Walls ate dinner at Kathy's house. Kathy's mother was a prostitute who always had food in the house, and upon eating all the meat off a chicken bone, Walls made this statement, almost forgetting that Ginnie-Sue, Kathy's mother, had brought home that chicken by selling her body, by putting herself in danger, by having her body severed from her identity for survival.

Jeannette Walls's own mother, while unhinged and unforgiving, was not a sex worker. Walls never had to watch her own mother sell her sex for food. Her connection to food and sex was through a stranger, a prostitute's ability to care for her kids, but this woman was not her mother. As hungry as I was as a child, no amount of chicken, roasted or otherwise, could make me tip my hat to an industry that rendered women invisible, erased, as they lay beneath men for food, for money, for anything that reduced them to objects of singular servility and self-abasement.

If I could pinpoint the exact moment in time, in childhood, that I became estranged from my body, the moment my mother admitted she had sex for food was it. It washed over me with the understanding that one woman's body could be used outside of her own pleasure. I concluded that if I didn't feel attached to my body, then it couldn't hurt me. If it didn't belong to me, then I wouldn't feel anything when someone else was using it the way I experienced men using my mother's body.

I don't think my mother offered her body out of her own choice. She had not prostituted herself before. Athanasia willingly gave sex to the men who came before Kristos. I remember the wanton way her hands coiled around the fisherman's neck, pulling him to her. That was desire, want, choice.

But when she brought the chicken to Kristos, she tossed it at him. There was no smile on her full lips when she said the words, "I did it." They were words that said, *Here, I did what you wanted. Eat your fucking chicken.* She sat next to him on the floor with some distance between them, and though I glued my eyes to her face, she did not look at me. Or him. Only at her hands, ringing the hem of her skirt around the knuckles of her thick, dirty fingers. Her shoulders were hunched, as if she had curled inside her own body for shelter like a turtle.

This is not the woman I feared when my father lived with us. Her body was no longer strong, lithe, heavy with pride and power. Curved and small, her body was now weak as it waited for Kristos to toss scraps of chicken flesh to her. She peeled the pink meat off the bone slowly, almost against her will.

My fear of her diminished at that moment, slinking tentatively toward the man I would fear for the rest of my life, even long after I left him behind in the tenements of Athens, Greece, capturing him in the faces of American men, my heartbeat pounding as if incessant sheets of rain dropped like sobs from the open sky, loud and unrelenting, every time a man, any man, raised his voice to me, stood too close to me, or towered over me.

With feet tucked beneath me, I could hear my stomach grumbling for the meal my mother's body purchased for us with her sex. It occurred to me then that I was on my own. I would have to protect myself, and I would have to protect my body with singular exhaustion and vigilance, because the once-powerful force that had been my mother was subdued by a man, by this one man who planned to stay for a long time. I trembled at the thought of what he could do to me, to the body that carried me, vulnerable, bony, and frail. I was in danger. Because of my body. Because its fragility could be used against me—to hurt me—and

I didn't know how to protect myself. I wasn't strong enough. Big enough. Clever enough to outsmart him.

My body, with its interminable needs, made me weak. Weak like my mother when the tables turned, and she found herself on her knees, Kristos's fists looming over her crumpled form. I hated it for its susceptibility because it cost me my freedom, my self-reliance. Even as young as I was back then, I was aware of the dangers of women relying on men for food, and more than anything, I loathed my body's hunger and how easily it yearned for the scraps Kristos threw at it, to pacify it, to make me indebted to him through my body.

My fingers reached out to grab the dregs of chicken he tossed in my direction, as if I were an animal. I willed my body to stop, to resist the hunger pangs as they knotted and squealed from inside of me. I told myself that I could find food for us the next day, but my fingers reached for the fleshy thigh bone and shoved it into my mouth. Ignoring my need to spit it out, my mouth clamped over it and bid my jaw to lock the food in place.

I owed him now. Kristos. I was his. My mother, my sister, and I belonged to him. If we took nothing from him, we owed him nothing. But we were too hungry, too weak to know better. To resist.

The combination of chicken and sex is when self-loathing was birthed in me. I can sketch the lines back to that moment, that struggle between my body's hunger and my will's resistance to being fed by and indebted to an evil man who threatened to sell my body as soon as I was old enough.

"I will teach you to be a woman. A good woman. Like your mother," Kristos promised me at night, whispering the words in my ear as I lay on the hard ground of empty buildings we fled at dawn, or on the soiled mattress we all shared once we found a small and cheap apartment to live in. He winked at me over my mother's bare shoulder, his hard, brown fingers caressing her bony clavicle, running a long, yellowed fingernail over her pale skin. He laughed when I clenched my jaw and turned my body away from him. My mother's snorts joined his mockery of me, a hollow, cackling sound that ripped me open at the seams, reminding me I would find no comfort in or protection from her.

I have starved my body in ways that wear it down each day, reminding it who is in control. I am. Not it. It's just a body, and I have erased any value the world, with its coarse men and sexist predilections, has assigned it. My body belongs only to me. And this is how it should be. The only way I can exist in a world that finds sex to be the only value women possess.

It will never belong to men like Kristos, who took ownership of my mother's body as if it were a one-room apartment he was renting out. He sold it to other men, making her stand on the street corners while he hailed down cars, shoved his head through open windows, bragging about my mother's tricks and skills, promising them a good time. When cash was exchanged, he opened the door of the car and let my mother inside, waving her off. Eleni and I hung around in the background, waiting for her to return. We sat on the corner of Athens' streets, the sun's rays beating against our faces with the unrelenting force I imagine my mother's johns used on her.

I came to know my mother as only a body, a feminine one with breasts and thighs and secrets between her legs that men sought, willing to pay cash for a few moments of being cradled by it, as if returning to the womb of the women who brought them into this world. What did their mothers teach them about women's bodies? What did their fathers teach them? Where do men learn that women's bodies are expendable, commodified, disembodied from the women who come attached to the skin and the bones bending beneath the weight of men's demands?

It is dangerous to be a woman. This is the earliest lesson I learned, and my body's existence confirms its victimization because it's not me that men have wanted. It's my body they have paid for in dinners and movies and drinks at the bar. My breasts and thighs and sex exist to them as if they are separate parts that could be used and consumed, clutched in male hands and eyes without my consent. These parts can be taken from me, while still attached to me, and I would have no say. No strength to fight men off, no right to keep what is mine.

How does that happen? How did it happen to my mother? Where was the monster I knew, whose brutality was fed by the weaknesses of her husband and children? There was only complacence now perched upon my mother's shoulders, like a muted songbird, its tongue cut off, a glaze of surrenders peeking out from its unblinking eyes.

Where does consent come into the picture of a sex worker with a pimp? He gives his consent for the consumption of her body, takes the cash, offers her services to strangers as if the body he serves belongs to him. It might as well belong to him. It no longer belonged to her, and her primary function was to use it to fill his pockets with money and power.

Watching her body, soft and bountiful, move beneath the weight of his own virile one, her arms forced above her head by fists that kept them pinned there, her face averted to the side, her eyes nebulous, as if she weren't even present, taught me the skill of leaving one's body behind during one's ravage. That the two could be separate, living apart, one seemingly unaffected by the other.

She modeled my first and earliest detachment between a girl and her body. After all, her body was not her own. It did not belong to her. It belonged to the men who sought her out for her tits and ass and paid her for them, scratching their groin on their way out. When you give your body away like that—to every set of hands and eyes and thighs that demand it and desire it and pay for it—how can it belong to you? How can you love it?

Sex has not been normal for me—easy or pleasurable. I have been deeply affected, scarred in places that fortify themselves against men and the pleasures they seek in women's bodies— with or without the woman being present or happy or fulfilled. Places that never allow me or my body pleasure, our desires muted and repressed by what we have seen and known. My life's battle has been to keep what's mine, my body enshrined in forced innocence, against its will, fortified against hands and mouths and penetrations that would render it used and foreign and not mine. An otherness that others would define and possess.

And I would rather die than let that happen.

(M)OTHERING GIRLS

*G*irls learn to perceive their bodies from their mothers.

This is at the root of the unhappy pairing between me and my body. Since I have had two mothers, I have two working models that define how I interact with the shame I carry with me wherever I go. But the first mother, Athanasia, is the one who taught me to fear my sexual body, to see its dangers and vulnerabilities, and I drew shame in shapes and scribbles all along my skin long before I could speak or write about it in words.

My birth mother starved my body long before I could fend for it. And in so many ways. She didn't feed us. Care for us. Touch us. Or love us. An angry and volatile woman, Athanasia had five children's bodies to feed, and mine was her fourth. By the time I came along, she was not around to defend us, shelter us, or feed us. She was too busy escaping her own pain, abandoning a home full of starving babies and a husband who married her for them.

It wasn't until my thirties that I found out her brother, Dimitri, arranged their marriage. He wanted her taken care of so he could marry the love of his life, Efthalia. But no one would have her.

At twenty, she was unhinged and volatile, muttering beneath her breath, a wild look in her eyes promising to unleash the rage that lived like a fiery dragon in her belly. My father, John, was older by twenty years and desperate to marry, to have a family. So he looked the other way, concentrating on her youth instead, on the rounded hips that bragged fertility and birthing rights, securing him with four children and five miscarriages in a little over a decade.

Her body was too busy to care for us, feeding its own hungers with an array of men who took her away from her family and returned her home late at night. My father was too weak to bar her from entering the home that he inherited when he married her. It was her bride price. He watched men drop her off outside of our home, his pallid and wasted features taking in her laughter, trickling fast and free like water gushing down a stream that stopped short as soon as she opened the door to our small home in Peristeri, a broken-down suburb in the poor part of Athens.

The woman who gave birth to me possessed a strong body. It was short and stout and full of power. Full of violence. This is how I came to know her body as a child inside my four-year-old trembling one, seated at the kitchen table beside my two older brothers, Stavros and Nikos, hands folded on my lap, eyes averted from the domestic storms of a childhood bathed in blood and gore.

Her fists pounded against my father's face, her knuckles drenched in his blood. Her legs, thick and muscular, kicked him in the stomach when he fell to the floor from the impact of her rampage. She laughed at him, at the tears filling up his eyes, a high-pitched screech rising from the pit of her taut stomach up to the full-breasted chest that heaved with fervor, past the throat canal that arched upward with self-satisfaction. I could tell even then that this power she had over my father—to pummel him, to make him cower to his knees, weeping like a child—was a surge of pride for her, a woman who never had much power to begin with.

She was the most formidable person I encountered in those days, until Kristos came into our lives, and watching a woman devour a man with her fists taught me that power has nothing to do with one's gender. Women aren't weak. They're not frail or the softer sex.

Power has to do with how much rage swells inside of us and how much of its monstrous torrents we allow to overwhelm us and those we care about, knocking us all down with an interminable force we can't overcome. Our bodies channel that rage, vibrating with its charge, helpless to its spasms and surges. We learn that the damage that remains gives us physical strength we hadn't ever imagined. Strength people told us we couldn't develop because of our sex and our diminutive size.

It must feel good, though, having such power, a lightning bolt expanding inside of you, tearing away the facade of flesh and bones that we have been told cannot compare to men's. I wouldn't know, but I imagine that's how my mother felt when she unfurled her wings of fury upon my father, a small, timid, tired man who didn't fight back.

He left instead.

The first memory I have held onto despite my adoptive mother's insistence that I forget was the day my father escaped his wife's abuse. I was four, and my two older brothers and I watched from the round kitchen table as my mother grabbed my father's head and brought it down hard against the corner of the stainless-steel sink. My brothers and I looked down in shame, tears flooding our eyes. We averted our gaze from the scene that took place only a few feet away from us and away from each other, biting our lips and praying for it to end. This brutality against our father was a common occurrence.

We knew better than to intervene. He was older, bigger than us, and we waited for him to muster up the courage he needed to fight back. To lash out. To punch her back.

But he never did. That kind of rage did not live in his bones.

His body slid to the floor instead, his fingers wiping the blood from the open gash on his forehead where the corner of the sink had sliced and separated the skin. My mother ran to their bedroom, a small space separated by a plastic partition with a door handle screwed to it, and returned with her red stiletto.

While my father was still on the floor, shaking his head from the shock of the impact, my mother lunged at him, released a high-pitched wail from her mouth, and stabbed him on his back with the sharp heel. When his body arched back in agony, she struck him again, this time on the corner of his left eye, blood spilling loosely, sliding down his cheeks, his mouth, the white lapel of his shirt, the bright red stain widening and expanding across the cotton fabric. A stain that would remain fixed and permanent in my memory bank, reminding me of the volatile roots of my childhood that not even adoption could reverse.

Covering his bloodied eye, my father cried out in pain and ran toward the front of the house. We heard him banging on the thin door of the home adjoining ours and belonging to our aunt Asimina, my mother's sister, who lived next to us.

While Nikos, my oldest brother and the second born, ran after him, Stavros and I remained in our seats, afraid of what would come next. We could hear our aunt open the door, gasp at the bloodied sight of our father, and pull him into the safe and quiet spaces of her own home.

"Oh, John! What has she done to you?" Pity peppered her words as she pulled him into her home and closed the door behind them.

He didn't return. He found refuge in his sister's arms and home, and she took care of him until he died of lymphoma, three years before I reunited with my family.

He didn't take us with him, either. He left without a word, and my brothers and I no longer had his body to stand between his wife's rages and our helplessness. Her hands showed us no love, no tenderness. Just roughness, five-fingered arrows darting toward our cheeks at the slightest provocation, staining our pale skin with scarlet strips of savagery.

My mother was a fury, her black hair tangled, dangling like

wild weeds about her weathered and menacing features. I often curled into my own body for shelter from her attacks, but it betrayed me with its quivering. It betrays me still when I am fearful or anxious, and it's one thing I loathe most about my body. This telling of tremulous fingers and weak-kneed impotence is often conveyed to my enemies. I wish my body would carry me with grace and strength, but I suppose it has as much to learn about tolerating me as I have about tolerating it.

My body is bent and fragile, like a plant with watered down roots, overwrought by a toxic environment that does not care for its health or potential. I continue to grow and thrive, breathing with force, bending and twisting with every gasping inhalation of polluted air surrounding me. My survival is forced because I know no other way.

My father's absence fractured what remained of our family. His leaving led to the loss of my brothers, Stavros and Nikos. I remember the last day I saw them, their thin frames holding them up with false pride, concealing the pain they felt in being put on a bus headed to an orphanage for boys, all of them neglected by their families either through death or poverty. It makes sense to me that school officials and social workers banded together and took them from my mother, who couldn't bother to feed us, or wash our clothing, or send us to school.

The same thing happened with my oldest sister, Maria, who was the first to tumble out of our mother's womb. She was born with club feet and fingers, her forehead long and wide enough that it did not match the Koutrogiannis kids' features. Her impediments resulted from the use of thalidomide, a drug prescribed to my mother for her nausea while Maria was in utero. My mother rejected her defects, leaving her in soiled sheets and diapers for hours, offering to sell her to the gypsies.

That's one scenario.

Another is that without my father around, my mother could

no longer feed extra mouths, so she sent Nikos and Stavros off as wards of the state. But she kept me and Eleni around. Because we were girls. Because we were the youngest. Because Kristos would prosper from us. From our sex.

Or perhaps she sent my brothers off to punish our father for not returning to us. After he left and refused to come back, my mother dressed us up, wiped the dirt off our faces, and took us to his job site. I remember that day, seeing his shoes crusted with dirt, the hem of his pants wrinkled and worn, the hands I adored, long, strong, veined, and familiar.

I ran to those hands, wrapped my arms around his thighs, and held my breath until I felt his fingers touch the top of my head. When they did, I inhaled the tobacco-filled scent of him, pushing my head deeper into the curved knuckles of his hands, as if my hair and his fingers were roots from the same tree, and when they recognized their kinship, that they belonged together, they would enmesh and entangle, becoming one strong, virile vine, surging with oxygen. Maybe even love.

But his fingers pulled away, and when I raised my eyes, I watched them quiver and shrink from me.

"You're not my daughter," he said to me in a husky voice I hadn't heard before. "You're not mine."

He walked away then, his back a crumbling wall of bones that began to wear away and disintegrate into the dirt and gravel still holding me up. I remained rooted to my spot, empty of him, like a gangrenous limb, amputated by force. My brothers pried me from the spot, pulling on my arms with agitation. They, too, were angry and abandoned. He left them behind as well. None of us had enough power and love to bring him back to us. We came with our mother, and he was willing to sacrifice his kids so as not to encounter her again.

I remember the day my mother and I walked my brothers to the bus stop, the day she sent them away. I waited between them, holding their hands, watching them shuffle their tattered shoes in the dirt, and then waving to them as their faces and bodies disappeared into the bus that would take them away and never bring them back. Following my mother back home, I knew nothing would ever be the same without them. I had no one older to watch out for me anymore.

A few months later, my mother gave birth to Eleni. Eleni was the fifth baby, but she wasn't my father's. Maybe that is why he left, too. Athanasia was pregnant with Eleni when my father deserted us. Stavros says Eleni belonged to the motorcycle man— who disappeared at the same time.

Eleni did not have our golden features, the blondish-brown hair and light-brown eyes we inherited from our father. She had ink-black hair and equally dark eyes that slanted like a cat's. Only four when she was born, I became a little mother to her, holding her in my arms, feeding her, soothing her whimpers before they turned into blistering cries threatening to pry open my own wounds, stifled sobs pouring out of me like unbound waterfalls. I was in charge of her while our mother fed sex to her johns and Kristos pocketed her earnings.

Tears didn't help in my world. They were just more weight, and I carried enough already. My baby sister. Losing my brothers. My father. Living with the man who took his place, keeping away from his hands and eyes and mouth when he demanded I kiss him on the lips. There was no room inside me for soft things like tears and longings. I braced myself only for strength, cold and hard and menacing to the touch.

I braced myself for the storm that was to come without forgiveness or reprieve. And all of it without my father. Without a whisper of his protection or gentleness. The only gentleness I had known as a child, that ironically, came from a man. My baba.

FATHERS AND PIMPS

Sexual hunger gnawed at my birth mother's insides. She had been taught by men, unfortunately, that her value rested in her sex. The only way she could express love or be loved was through sex. I did not grow up with pangs of desire for sexual coupling. Men do not hold the answer for me, the missing piece that fits perfectly, lovingly into the chasms of my own longings.

My own hungers lie in love. I long to be loved. To feel loved. It's the thing I never got. And the only thing I've ever wanted. To be mothered and loved and cared for. Although I found this in Richard, after a while, it faded, and I am learning men's love is not maternal, not present unless sex also accompanies it. Men cannot love me the way I want them to, without sex, without transactional purpose.

I am more like my adoptive mother, Ann, in this. She was closed off to men, to sex, to love even. The only people in her life that she loved were her parents. When they died, months apart from one another, Ann attempted to recapture that love by becoming a mother. Since she was too haughty and thought herself above the likes of men, often mocking their existence and pseudo self-importance, adoption was the only way for her to be a mother, to love without giving one inch of herself, her body, or her heart.

I have learned from her how to stop love from entering my body, how to shut off the valves of feeling with the ease of twisting a pipe's knob when the toilet water overflows and promises to spill soiled liquids onto the floor, the carpet, the scale used to weigh the emotional baggage strapped to the squishy parts of my stomach, calling itself stress, anxiety, depression, or just plain old aloneness.

In comparing my two mothers, Ann, the second mother, afflicted with equal parts narcissism and self-assertion, is the one I respect. I emulate her, not in all things, but in independence and self-repression. Both were faulty maternal beings, but as women, Athanasia was more malignant than Ann in defining femininity and womanhood for me.

The asexual parts of Ann spoke to me of power and self-determination outside of a woman's dependence on men. And this was a radical perspective of female independence in the seventies, but a most profound difference I needed to help me see that not all women needed men to survive life. Not all women relied on their sex to make men happy or to find an equal footing in a world that consistently placed women beneath men and children. There were some women who did not use their sex at all. Like Ann.

This was an important lesson for me as a girl child, especially once Kristos, my first mother's pimp, kicked in the doors with his black boot and entered our lives as if he owned us.

I don't know or remember where he came from. The first time my birth mother brought him home is not a memory I hold close to my chest, and after years of being silenced by my adoptive mother, who didn't want to hear about the people or life I led before she took me, I don't hold many memories of him.

The few memories I have held onto, perhaps to remind me of the dangers I can find myself in as a girl, a woman, are fragmented assertions of power and conflict between an adult man and a little girl. The winner was obvious to everyone but me, and whenever it came to him, I mouthed off like an unwitting fool.

In one recollection, I see him grabbing me by the throat, lifting me up off the floor, and pinning me against the wall. He brought his face close to mine, so close that I could smell the sourness of his breath as he gritted his teeth and cursed me out. I think he cursed me out. I don't remember many words between us. Only a few. And they came later, when I was older, and my memories were more inclined to stick. He was angry, his knuckles digging into my throat, my mother screaming at him to put me down, to let me go. I removed my gaze from his, only to collect the image of her pounding her fists against his back until he let go and watched me drop to the floor with a small thump. He eyed me for a bit, for good measure I'm sure, and then stormed off.

"You're not my baba," is the refrain of my childhood's song. I spit the words at him every chance I got. He slammed his boombox against my head every chance he got, reminding me of my place as a child, a girl, overtaken by a force I was too small and too young and too unprotected to match.

I was four when Kristos took his place at the head of our family, when he displaced my father and the quietude I found only in him, in the palms of his hands as they touched the top of my head, massaging calmness into my thoughts with just his fingertips. This is how I remember my father. He was soft and good. And weak, yes, but not all men are born hostile and loud and brash. My baba was the opposite, and I loved him for it.

And I hated him. For leaving us. For not taking us with him. For forcing us to navigate the formative years of our childhood splintered from each other. For telling me I wasn't his *kori*. His daughter. For not knowing, or caring, that when he left, another man, quite unlike him, would join our mother and drag us to the ends of debauchery and corruption.

My baba was safe after he left, cared for by a doting sister while his children were separated and cared for by strangers not invested in their mental or emotional health. He was an abandoner. A deserter. And yet, I would have given anything for one more moment with a man like him to remind me I could find goodness and safety in men.

I knew who my father was. And it wasn't the vile, greasy-haired man who made his money as a nomad, a gypsy, selling women for food, for drachmas, promising to make similar women out of their daughters. Daughters who did not belong to him but to the women he exploited with his masculine prowess, iron fists, a hollow laugh that chased me in my sleep and ingrained in me a fear of men that splintered like dried-up wood in my chest, getting caught on my skin, pinching and tearing at my insides.

Or maybe it was the memory of waking up next to him, his body sweaty and naked on the yellowed mattress Eleni and I shared with him and our mother.

I developed a habit of waking up early, so as not to have him roll over me, his legs and arms spooning my smaller frame. Often, I placed Eleni's little body between us, like a stanchion, so I could close my eyes and sleep without fearing his closeness. I spent early mornings cleaning the kitchen, sweeping the floor, wiping the countertop, folding clothes and putting them away, throwing out food cartons and leftover meals in the garbage. Keeping the small space of our one-room apartment free of dirt and chaos helped me breathe easier, without choking on the fractured bones of my family's demise.

And then one morning, he wanted me to kiss him on the mouth.

"No," I fumed at him, heat rising from my chest and finding root in my throat.

"Come now," he flicked his cigarette ash at me, a threat of what would come if I didn't obey.

"No." I dug my heels into the ceramic floor that held me up, my knees buckling beneath the weight of my fear and his demand. A demand I knew I would eventually have to serve.

"Give your baba a kiss, already," my mother snapped at me, reaching over on the mattress and snatching the cigarette from his fingers. She took a long drag and watched me as the smoke escaped her lips and nose. "He won't quit until you do what he says."

I forced my feet to move toward them and positioned my face a few feet away from his. He laughed, the acrid, decaying scent of his breath forcing my nose and mouth to clamp shut. He grabbed both sides of my face and pulled me to him, his wet mouth, open and foul, meeting my zipped lips. The more I tried to wriggle free, the more he held me there, his eyes open, his mouth laughing into mine.

He locked me in that position until I no longer resisted him, my body still and forgotten and unable to hold its breath another second. When he finally let go, I stared right into his smirking gaze, took the dishrag still in my grasp, murky and rank from my earlier cleaning of the kitchen sink, and made a ceremony of wiping it across my mouth. I ran out of the apartment, spit the taste of him into the dirt, and dragged clean air into my lungs like a heavy smoker, hoping it would erase the stench of his breath and the feel of his lips on mine, drown out the spasms of their uncontrollable laughter still echoing and vibrating against the bones of my body.

The last time I saw him as a child was the day police officers rounded me and my mother and Eleni to the station in search of him.

"Where is he?" the police officer asked my mother. "We want to ask him some questions."

"Bah!" My mother waved him off as if he were a fly invading her nostrils or eye sockets. She turned her face away from him, licking her finger and wiping a pretend smudge of dirt off my baby sister's forehead.

"I know where he is," I piped up, seeing this as my opportunity to rid us of the man who threatened to make me into a good woman, like my mother.

My mother kicked me with her free leg, the one that didn't have Eleni's slight frame perched on it, sucking her thumb and watching us with curiosity.

"He's at our home right now," I said, smiling at the officer who was taking a keen interest in the cuts and scrapes on my arm—bloody scratches I received from the stray cats my mother collected that fought me for scraps of whored out chicken.

I gave him our address, and as he bent his head to write it down on a piece of paper, I flipped a satisfied smile toward my mother as if it were the middle finger. She reached out and planted a five-fingered handprint on my cheek. But it didn't wipe away my smile, as she expected.

Joy rose from the tips of my toes to my chest like a vibrant heatwave that warmed all the parts of my body gone untouched, unloved, and unfed. I felt full for the first time in years, taking this one scrap of courage with me to my new home in America to remind me of the day I changed the events of my life with a single act of bravery. And the power that came with using my voice.

When we returned home a few hours later, the place was in disarray, and Kristos was gone. They had arrested him.

A man like that, though, doesn't just disappear. He stayed with me. He comes for me in my dreams, like polluted fog, quiet and still, barely discernible until I am surrendered in its fold, blinded by its thickness. I don't know he is near me, affecting me, until it is too late.

He followed me to America. For a long time in my childhood, after my adoption, he surfaced in my dreams. I forced myself awake to make him disappear. In my dreams, I was in constant battle with him. I was small and ferocious, straddling him beneath the slight weight of my body and clenching my bony knees into his sides so he couldn't move. I lunged at him, throwing punches in his face with force and power I could only muster in my nightmares.

But all my punches landed softly, no matter how much weight I put into them. How much hatred and loathing I stuffed behind each strike. Every time my fists touched the brown skin of his face, his nose, his forehead, his cheeks, they did so without power. They bounced off, and I tried again. And again. And again. But still nothing.

Nothing but his laughter echoing in my ears, riling me up even more. Mocking my insignificance. I was a little girl. In my dreams or in real life, I was no match for a man. Any man.

One of the most vivid dreams I had as a child while living with Ann stuck with me. In this dream, I was in a school building that housed only girls. There was a rapist on the campus, and girls were screaming as they fled from their dorms and sought escape in the gardens of the quad. I was among these girls, running blindly in the dark, in my sheer nightgown, unaware of my surroundings.

He jumped me, a dark-clad figure without a face or voice. He climbed on top of me, straddled me, tore my nightgown off so that I lay beneath him naked, and stabbed me in that tender place between my thighs.

Then he was gone. Just like that. I stood up slowly, trembling against the chill in the air, the blood spilling from my open wound.

As I tried to gain my balance and figure out what to do, he attacked me again. But this time, I resisted. I pushed back.

"You can't kill me!" I screamed at him. I pointed to the blood slowly pouring out of the gaping gash his knife seared between my legs. "You see? I'm already dead."

I found him during the days of my American childhood as well. He was in the faces of men who whistled at me when I walked to school. He was in the neighborhood lecher who came to our school at three in the afternoon and pulled his coat away from his body so we could see his bare penis.

He was in the movies I watched, like *Grease*, resembling John Travolta with his sleazy demeanor, slicked-back hair, and seventies sideburns. Sideburns triggered me, but if they came attached to men with aggressive behaviors and sexual prowess, like Kristos, they invited an array of emotions from me that extended from fear to anxiety to rage within seconds.

Kristos came to me in songs, too. When Roy Orbison's "Pretty Woman" traveled through the airwaves of my radio or the car stereo, my skin chilled, and the bones that held me together got so rigid I thought my body would snap in half. This was the song that played on his boombox. The one he slammed against my face and head to shut me up. This was the song he used to sell my mother. She was a pretty woman, walking down the street. *How much do you want for her?*

And yes, if you're wondering, I did watch the movie *Pretty Woman*. When I was older, and I taught myself to detach from a childhood that no longer fit me or my new life as the American adoptee of a high school science teacher. As her daughter, I sat in the theater next to my childhood friend, Joyce, and watched the movie as a love story about a prostitute who believed she was worthy of operas and rubies and wealthy bachelors. Of love. Of respect.

But she wasn't the prostitute of my childhood.

My mother wasn't pretty or sexy. She didn't sell her body in a fictionalized, made-for-screen film that romanticized prostitution. She didn't have the choice of selling her body for her own survival until someone rescued her. She didn't have that kind of power or autonomy. She had a pimp, and he sold her sex for his survival. He hit her; he raped her; he took her house and rented it out for extra money; and he threatened her daughters, in front of her, for control.

There was no love in her prostitution. No john who would stop long enough to fall in love with her, honor her, and offer her a life without servitude to the masses.

Johns don't save whores. They use them. They pay for detached sex, and sometimes violence, and then they go home to their wives. They already have their happy-ever-afters.

Whores, not so much.

UnHINGED, UnNATURAL, UnMOTHER

I saw Kristos one more time.

It was in December 1999, five months after I married Richard. I returned to Greece to reunite with my siblings, or at least the ones I located through the Greek Embassy in Manhattan, Eleni and Stavros.

I was thirty years old and hadn't seen them since my adoption when I was eight. The five days I spent in Athens were emotional and included seeing everyone who had lived inside my head for the past twenty-two years. It was like holding up faded, yellowed images from a distant life, trying to name faces and recollect how they belonged to me in the childhood Ann had forced me to surrender so many years earlier. There were aunts and uncles and cousins, but more important to me were my siblings.

Although my father had died three years earlier from lymphoma, I wanted to see my mother, to wash away the debris my childhood kept spilling into my adult life, my marriage, my well-being. Before seeing her, however, my family thought it would be important to explain her to me. After all, the portrait of the woman I knew as my mother was limited to a child's understanding.

I did not come to know her—about her—the way most kids grow in their learning of their parents, acquiring a more complete picture of them as they get older and more cognizant of life's interferences and hardships. My memories of her were steeped in violence and shame. She was abusive. A prostitute. A child abandoner. But there was more to her, they told me. Her sister, Asimina, wanted me to know the full story of the woman who birthed me.

"Her father, your grandfather, was abusive," my cousins began telling me in Greek. We were all sitting in a circle, facing each other, in my aunt Asimina's home. The same home that was attached to the one I grew up in. The same home I often sought refuge and food in when my parents were fighting or when there was no one in my house to watch me or feed me.

I spent many days in this living room, small but warm and homey, eating Greek fries and *keftedes* and *horiatiki* salad with ripe tomatoes, red onions, and feta cheese, mesmerized by the moving images of their television set, my cousins often seated beside me on the living room floor. This time, I was amid my siblings and my aunt, as well as my cousins and their children.

"He beat his wife, your grandmother, and he killed a man in a bar fight. Like always, he was drunk. When they arrested and imprisoned him, your grandmother got sick and died shortly after. Their three children were separated and sent off to work. In those days, they lived in the homes in which they worked and were treated like servants," George, my cousin's husband, told me in English. He was the only one who spoke the language fluently, and since my Greek comprised an eight-year-old's vocabulary, we all relied on him to translate.

There was a pause. I nodded for him to continue.

"Your mother was only four or five. It was quite common for girls—without protection or parents around—to be raped. Your mother was, for many years, and by the time her brother, Dimitri, found her, she had been irreparably harmed."

"What do you mean?" I asked, grabbing Richard's hand for comfort.

"Your mother's not all there. By the time she married your father, she was slightly off, mentally."

"You're saying she is crazy?"

"She is . . . off. She knows what's going on around her, but her mind and thoughts go in and out. Her experiences affected her. You'll see tomorrow when you see her."

I looked at my sister, Eleni, whom I left behind so many years ago. My family took me from her and my mother and Kristos and put me on a plane to experience the American Dream every immigrant seeks. Unlike my siblings, I had a fairy godmother who plucked my roots from the tattered soil of our childhood and re-planted them in the plush gardens and rich earth of an American woman with a secure job, home, and mental state.

Our family did not put Eleni up for adoption. She stayed behind with our mother, who went from man to man, from bed to bed, until Eleni, too, was taken away and placed in an orphanage. Like the rest of us. The difference between my experience at the orphanage and theirs is they stayed until their eighteenth birthday. My aunt put me up for adoption. A stark difference for us all.

"You escaped," Eleni told me the first day I met her at our hotel, the Grande Bretagne in Syntagma Square. "I did not get to escape. To go off to America. To get a new family." There is a sea of resentment I cannot wade through to comfort her losses. My adoption spared me her life, her poverty. America raised me, and I learned that anything was possible for girls like us.

"Do you think our mother's crazy?" I asked, looking into her pained eyes, our cousins nodding their heads in unison.

"No," she shook her head. "She knows what she's done."

Arguing ensued in Greek, my native tongue. I should have understood, but their mouths moved quickly, and the words came out in bursts of garbled phrases I couldn't grasp long enough to comprehend. I caught a word here or there, but nothing made sense to me. I could only read emotions on the faces of these strangers, tied to me only by blood and vague memories.

There was anger and disgust on Eleni's features as she railed about our mother's neglect and abuse. There was compassion in the weathered features of my aunt, my mother's sister, also abandoned and sent off to indentured service. But she had come out of it fine. Married a lovely man who loved her and helped her raise three bright and successful daughters.

Why was my mother's journey so different? Why was it so mangled and chaotic?

"Your mother had a terrible time," my aunt Asimina said in defense of her only sister. "Our father raped her when he got out of jail. She told me a few years later, and I believed her." She dabbed at the tears rolling out of her eyes, black-gray hues of wrinkled skin sagging beneath them that spoke of a hard-lived life.

My gaze traveled across the room to find Stavros's brown, bulbous eyes. He shrugged his shoulders at me, took a long drag from his cigarette, blew smoke out of his nostrils, and said, "She's crazy. But I don't care. I won't come with you to see her."

He hadn't seen our mother since the day she and I walked him and Nikos to the bus that took them away from us and placed them in an orphanage to be raised by strangers. He was six then, and Nikos was eight. Nikos lived in Crete, and we planned to see him a few days later. They chose our father over her, and neither desired a relationship with our mother.

"I have to see for myself," I told them. An outsider, I could be objective and observe from a distance. There was no anger in me. I didn't possess either Stavros's or Eleni's resentments or Asimina's compassion for a woman I left when I was eight. Nothing lived in me except curiosity.

When the day came to meet my mother, Eleni, Richard, and I walked along a huge, empty lot somewhere in Athens. At this point of the trip, I was in a haze, and the city circled around me like a cloud storm of disconnected sounds and sights that made no sense. I was blind and happy to be led by Eleni, who crooked her arm through mine and pulled me from home to home, from bus to bus, from corner to corner to the lot my mother lived in. It was closed off by a three-foot metallic gate and guarded by four mangy-looking dogs. Teeth and ribs bared, they trotted back and forth along the inside of the crude fence, their growls outlining sharp fangs meant to rebuke and ward off trespassers.

Athanasia lived in the abandoned lot enclosed by the gate, protected by the dogs, amid an infinite collection of wreckage and debris. An old, abandoned truck sat on the far right, granting my mother and Kristos, the man who had terrorized me as a child, a niche of protection from the December winds and rain. To the left, they set an endless trail of cardboard boxes to create crude roofing, and alongside it, there were heaps of discarded clothing, food, blankets, and even scraps of furniture. Whatever one can toss away found a purpose in the lot my mother and Kristos called their home.

The woman who had given birth to me and made the first eight years of my life turbulent appeared to me for the first time in over twenty years. Her steps were deliberate and unhurried as she made her way toward us from the opposite side of the fence separating us. She was small in stature, no more than five feet tall, yet she commanded submission as she hushed the growling dogs. One order from her lips and they ceased their snarling assault. They yelped and whined and lay down quietly by her feet with the fearful obedience she had once imposed upon her children.

"Mama," Eleni addressed her with formality and detachment. "Do you know who this is?"

"Of course. Marina," she said, calling me by my given name. She was prepared for me, Eleni told me earlier. My uncle Dimitri, her brother, whom we visited the night before, told her I would be visiting.

"Come, come," said my mother, surveying me with a couple of quick glances. "Come into my happy home."

I clung to Richard's arm with an inflexible grip of steel. I needed to be grounded; I felt light and dizzy. The way I recall myself—and my body—in childhood. Tight and tethered, a blur of chaos threatening to overcome me.

My mother led us toward the center of the lot where her makeshift home was assembled, a collage of waste. This is how she had lived for over twenty years, without walls, a roof, children, bills, or responsibilities to fence her in. She lived out in the open with the Athenian sun, rain, and wind striking her face and giving it a weathered look, her skin a smooth layer of dark-tanned leather. Loose black-and-gray strands of hair escaped from beneath the red cap with YAMAHA inscribed on it. A hat a tourist had thrown away or lost. She wore baggy, dirty slacks, tattered shoes, and three layers of shirts on her back, beneath a mossy-green winter jacket with a broken zipper. Despite her poverty, two elegant gold rings adorned the pinky and wedding finger of her left hand, and I wondered if my father had given them to her.

With only a cursory glance, no one could have put together that we were mother and daughter. Not unless they looked closely, paying attention to minute details. Unlike my straight, light-brown hair, hers was nappy, unwashed, uncombed, and jet-black, the color of Eleni's hair. The similarities began and ended with the symmetrical lines that etched our features, large, oval brown eyes, and the wrinkled skin that folded beneath them when we smiled or squinted. Our faces reflected the identical curved lines that traveled from the side of our noses down toward our mouths. Our skin creased in the same places on our cheeks when we smiled or laughed, but that is where our likeness ended. I released a sigh of relief.

"This is the living room," my mother said, pointing toward

the center of the lot where a little fire was brewing on the hard soil of the ground.

"Kristos," she bellowed to the man I had hated as a child, her partner, lover, and pimp for the past twenty years. "Put some more wood on the fire for the kids. It's too cold for them out here."

"You remember your baba, Kristos?" She looked at me but pointed toward the wayward man sitting by the fire, smoking a cigarette. *He's not my father*, I remember seething as a little girl. I stood mute before him.

He was a foot taller than my mother and wore a white base-ball cap atop his own long, unkempt black-and-silver coils of hair that interlocked into greasy dreads. An equally untidy and nappy beard of salt-and-pepper curls covered his face. The only features I could view clearly were his hollow eyes, the dark color of his skin and hair, and the crooked nose that fanned out across the width of his face.

I looked at him and said nothing. He nodded his head at me, but the tension between us was solid, impenetrable. I had imag-ined this day for years, but now that it was here, I was at a loss for words.

I said nothing, watching him watch me from beneath his hooded lids and behind the heavy smoke that clouded his face. As I stole glances at him, I was surprised at how much he had changed. He no longer possessed the look of the formidable devil who had slammed his radio against my head when I was less than six years old. He no longer looked like the menacing man who had pushed me violently against the wall, his knuckles digging into my throat, stifling my rebellion.

Looking at him through the eyes of a thirty-year-old woman, he appeared to me small and innocuous. His power over me had dissolved with time, with this one and only meeting that finally closed the horror-based chapter we once shared.

I still wanted to know if he had abused me. My body acted as if he had, even though I couldn't remember. I thought seeing him would cement me in some concrete memory that would explain my inability to be intimate, my distrust of men, my need to scrub the memory of male eyes and hands off my skin after a night of forgetting myself, clamping my lids shut so I could feel rather than abandon the idea of being touched by a man. Richard was the only one I felt safe with back then. When he touched me, I didn't have to scrub him off. I didn't hate myself after sex with him, what little sex we did have.

But nothing came. No memories but the ones I had kept through my childhood and packed into my suitcase for this trip. Only silence hummed between us—a thick, loud, overbearing hum that muted out what was unsaid. It's as if we were both trying to figure out what the other remembered. But remembered what? Every memory I kept of him was full of anger and violence, and my nightmares about him centered on vengeance. Me punching him. Me hurting him. My fists bouncing off the wall of his chest in slow motion, with no impact, his laughter booming in my ears. Him stabbing me, blood dripping from the blade, scorching the insides of my thighs. In all my dreams of him, he had the power, and I had none.

As we sized each other up in silence, I wondered which memory of me he was recounting. Was it the way I mouthed off to him every time he told me to call him *Baba*? Or was it the time he kissed me on the mouth, and I spit the taste of him out? I couldn't know. I didn't ask. I found no words to say to him. To either of them. I only smiled, stupidly, and stood before them, paralyzed and silent.

Yawning away the memories of Kristos as if they bored me, I shifted my gaze toward Eleni, finding comfort in the little sister I abandoned when we were little. When I first contacted her, I was slightly disappointed that we did not resemble one another.

Richard and his sisters all look alike, and when they are in a room, everyone can tell they share the same Irish and Italian genes that come with red in their hair and blue or hazel in their eyes. Having grown up on my own and resembling no one, I so desperately wanted to look like someone. Knowing that I had a family with the same DNA so far away from me, I often wondered who I looked like.

When I dreamed of meeting my sister after all these years, I anticipated she would look like me. I expected to see myself in her eyes, in her nose, in her smile — anywhere. I wanted to belong to her and have her belong to me in a physical, traceable way. But we looked nothing alike. She was tall and big-boned with long, black hair, a heart-shaped face, a straight nose, pale white skin, and beautifully shaped dark eyes. She was fashionably dressed in a tight outfit with a red leather jacket and matching shoes and bag. She was very stylish, and I smiled, knowing that despite her hard life, she had fared well as an adult.

While Eleni tried to unscramble the puzzle behind our mother's rhetoric in order to translate it for me, Richard elbowed me out of my reverie, urging me to speak to my mother and ask her all the questions I had saved for her. I couldn't do it. My body was stuck in place, in time, in silence. Paralyzed by the scene that played out before me, I felt as if I were in the audience, watching a movie or documentary on a day in the life of the homeless. My body was present, but my mind was outside of me, watching from afar. Disconnected from my surroundings while existing within them simultaneously, my body and I were in sync — both dumb and awe-struck.

I took pictures instead, freezing the surrounding images and hoping that when I returned home, I could look at them and digest them with longing, not loss. Understand all the nuances that I couldn't grasp while in the moment. Through the safety of my camera lens, my eyes filled with the empty lot my mother re-

ferred to as her home and everything else within its spaces that
encapsulated her life.

There was the tightly bundled corpse of a dead dog my
mother had lovingly placed atop her cardboard home, unable to
bury its remains.

Click.

There were the relentless whines, yelps and squeals of nine
dogs running around us, their ribs protruding from the flea-in-
fested hair that clung to their coarse and scarred skin.

Click.

There was the sight of clean animal bones scattered upon the
dirt by the fire, making me wonder if they collected these dogs to
eat them.

Click.

There was the strange realization that the bizarre woman
standing before me, unabashed, making jokes about her life with
a radiant smile on her face, was my mother.

Click.

"If you need to pee, the bathroom is right there," my mother
informed us, lightheartedly pointing to a grassy area between the
truck and a mound of metal and cardboard scraps.

Click.

"Do you see this, Kristos?" she called out to the short, stout
man concealed by a thick cloud of smoke. "My daughters are
beautiful. Just look at them."

He grumbled a vague response from under the fumes of his
cigarette and said no more. I felt his eyes on me but refused to
look at him. Instead, I smiled appropriately and let Eleni do the
talking. I stood among them, swaddled like a baby in the folds of
silence, and swallowed the bile of what I had escaped.

I lost much of what they said to me. Their Greek was fast,
jumbled, and full of emotion. My sister spoke to our mother with
irritation dripping from her lips. Observing Eleni openly scoff at

her, I recognized the pain and unhealed wounds for which she held Athanasia accountable.

The last child to experience our mother's mad mothering, Eleni, like the rest of us, found refuge in an orphanage. When they released her on her eighteenth birthday, she told me the first night we met, she set out to find the mother from whom she fled when she was eight. She discovered Athanasia sitting on the curb on a random street in Peristeri, the same neighborhood that had birthed us. Our mother was homeless, a beggar, her calloused, outstretched hands cradling loose drachmas that afforded her coffee or cigarettes, two of her minor vices. With barely enough money in her own pockets, Eleni offered to buy her lunch. As they walked and made small talk, a car approached them and slowed down. An older man popped his head out of the window and acknowledged our mother.

"This is my daughter," my mother told him. "She's a beauty, no?"

The man laughed aloud and nodded; his false teeth stretched into a sheepish grin.

"Does she want to go for a ride?" He gave Athanasia a knowing look. Eleni didn't miss it. Our mother never kept that part of her life a secret from her children.

"Why not?" my mother replied. "How much do you want for her?"

That day, Eleni walked away from our mother and refused to turn back. It was not until six years later, when I came into the picture needing to know what she already learned about the woman who had shattered our childhood, that Eleni saw her again. Taking me to see our mother was not a trip Eleni wanted to make, but she understood my desire to meet her and made the arrangements.

I caught my birth mother's features shifting from one expression to the next, mesmerized by the foreign woman who damaged every child to whom she gave life. Fascinated by their tenuous mother-and-daughter exchange, I recalled the same distorted face of resentment that had held me captive as a child, for I too had once loathed the maddening creature now standing before me, smiling at me, her mouth spitting out Greek words and phrases I was too slow to catch.

I realized she was an unfamiliar person for whom I harbored no feelings, good or bad. Any trace of hatred I nursed toward the woman standing before me, looking at me without shame or accountability, had been replaced by fears of abandonment and rejection. I understood Eleni's resentment for our mother, not because I shared that resentment, but because I often felt the same way toward the woman who had raised me. Not my birth mother, from whom I was severed like an amputated limb, but my adoptive mother, who made it almost impossible for me to reattach, since my parts did not fit into any of hers in the ways she and I expected.

Although I spent the formative years of my childhood detesting the mother who was irreparably neglectful of our most basic needs and reckless with our childhoods, my experiences with her ended when I was eight. After my adoption, I didn't have to see her again. The bitterness attached to my unmet needs, like a second strip of uncomfortable skin, exists not for her, but for Ann. My anger toward her is still sharp and tense, like a live wire shrieking with agitation whenever she speaks. Or chews. Or laughs. Or breathes in the spaces I am forced to share with her.

Aware of the strain that aggravated Eleni's demeanor toward Athanasia and aware that there was no anger reserved inside me for my birth mother, a wave of sadness washed over me. I was a stranger to the conflicts that existed between them—between all the members of my blood family and the discord they shared. I was out of place among them and their pain. There was an ocean of distance that separated me from the rest of them, and despite the rekindling I initiated, I recognized myself as an outlier once again.

The family I had yearned for all these years and been kept away from continued to exist without me, without pause, as if my absence had no impact on their lives. It only made me an outsider, and not even my presence could make me part of their discordant unit. I was a guest, invited to visit a family I had not known or seen in over two decades. A polite smile swept over my face, and I surveyed them from a distance as mother and daughter attempted to unravel the stubborn tangles of their irreparable bond.

"You think I was bad?" our mother snorted at Eleni. "Your father was no better. He was not the saint everyone thought he was. He had a woman on the side, and he had children with her. She was a *putana*. Oh, he wasn't much of a saint, that one," she said to us, trying to get us on her side.

I tossed Eleni a quizzical glance, my eyebrows arched, and my eyes lit up with realization. My mother was talking about herself. She was the woman on the side who had children with him. She was the prostitute. There was no other woman. At some point in her life, probably before she married our father, she had detached from her own experiences, like a lone reed expunged from a field of grass, loosened and carried away by a gust of wind that was more powerful than the tattered tendrils of her roots.

My mother came closer to me and looked me straight in the eyes. I could feel the warm touch of her breath on my cheeks and my body's desire to reject her closeness. I am not one for physical touch or for sharing physical space, but I forced my body not to move a muscle. I planted my feet into the firm ground beneath me and stood still, not wanting to insult her.

A long sigh of resignation rose inside me, heaving like a

dead weight against my chest. Looking at the woman who was supposed to have been my mother, I realized that no accurate depictions of the past would come from her. She was not only a mystery to me but also to herself. Eleni waved at my mother's words with impatience and told her I didn't remember much of my childhood.

Kristos looked up and took a long drag from his cigarette.

"Look, *Mana mou*," he urged her, referring to her as his woman. "Don't dredge up things the girl doesn't remember. It's better that she doesn't remember them, anyway."

My eyes scoured his face for a few seconds, longer than I wanted. He remembered more about my childhood than I did. I wondered what he didn't want me to recall. I wanted to use my voice, but my jaw had wired itself shut. Maybe it is better that I don't remember, as everyone in my family believes. Maybe I don't want to remember it all. The memories I have held onto are enough. Maybe even too much.

"Bah!" my mother grumbled, dismissing him with a quick jerk of her hand.

When the time came to leave, Athanasia walked us to the gate, her loyal dogs trailing us. They sat quietly by her feet when she stopped to pull back the short gate so that Eleni, Richard, and I could exit her crude abode.

"Come," my mother said as she reached for me. "Give your mama a kiss."

I moved into her space and kissed her on one cheek and then the other, careful not to touch the open pink sore that marked her right cheek.

I walked away without a backward glance. It was the first time I had seen my birth mother in over twenty years, and it was the last. I have returned to Greece three times since and have not attempted to see her. I took enough pictures of her and her home to last me the rest of my life, and in all of them, a wide and jovial grin stuck to my face, reminding me of the surreal events of that day.

The funny thing is, I haven't looked at them since the time it took me to paste them into a photo album. The album has collected dust and aged, stuffed into the back of the closet where all my other albums sit from my travels, my wedding, the birth of my children, my recent trips to Greece to visit Eleni and Stavros. I open those, but I can't make myself open the one that recalls my visit with my mother.

It's like that small flower area in my backyard, when my back was to the pool and my daughter, then four years old, almost drowned. I was planting rose bushes and didn't hear her small frame fall into the water and go under. It was my son's screams that woke me from my stupor, the sound of Richard's body crashing through the surface of the water to pull her out that made me slowly turn around and find her little body, drenched and trembling, being carried toward me. Even then, my body froze, the only signs of life coming from the pulsing throb of my heart as it quickened and crashed against my chest cavity.

I watched from a distance until I was sure she was breathing, then grabbed her, took her inside to dry her, and did not look back at the place where the rose bushes were planted.

I know the exact spot where she fell in and struggled for breath. The exact spot I stood upon when she went down, and I froze.

The idea of returning to the album with my mother's laughing face amid the debris of her life is like that. I know where it is, but I avoid it just the same.

AN OUTLIER

The path to my adoption began with my role in having Kristos arrested. It was my reward. Or my punishment. It all depends on how you look at it. How you interpret fate. Or chance, perhaps.

A few days after Kristos's arrest, my mother tossed my few possessions into a plastic bag and took me to her brother's construction site, which he owned and managed.

"You have to take her," she pleaded with my uncle Dimitri and his wife, Efthalia. "I can't take care of her. Kristos is in jail, and I have enough to do with Eleni."

"We'll take her," my aunt said, smiling down at me, her soft brown eyes in contrast with the blond tendrils that whispered softly about her rounded face. "For as long as you need us to."

As they spoke, I took Eleni, who was between two and three years old, a few feet away.

"Let's play hide-and-go seek," I told her. She nodded, her smile wide, her ink-black hair, long and tangled, swishing around her head. "Shut your eyes then, and I'll count to ten."

She closed her cat-shaped eyes, oval and slanted, but when she opened them, I wasn't there. I ran away from her, the only way I could think to leave her behind without feeling guilty or complicit in her abandonment. It was a cruel way to leave her, but I was just a child, and I was ready to leave my mother. I was afraid Kristos would come back and learn that I was responsible for his arrest. I didn't want to know what the consequences would be.

As I have gotten older, I realize now that I was just like my father. We both ran away. Both escaped Athanasia, leaving behind the pain and chaos her existence unearthed and the little people who were scorched by the untamed fires she left in her wake.

I abandoned Eleni in such a traumatic way that when she opened her eyes, I was nowhere to be found. I had already moved on. Without her. She wouldn't see me again until I was thirty, and she was twenty-six. But I was only six, and all I wanted at six was anything other than my mother. And Kristos. And johns. And caring for a toddler when I could hardly care for myself.

I loved my new freedom away from my mother. But only because it came with my aunt Efthalia. Despite only staying with her for a year, I don't regret my time with her and her family. She was a gentle woman, a doting mother. I think she loved me, and I imagine that there would be no child on earth that she couldn't love. She bathed me, spent the time needed to rid me of hair lice and bad memories. She fed me food and love and kindness until I was full and sated.

"*Agapi mou*," she said, tucking me into the first bed I slept in without having to share it with Kristos, with my mother, with Eleni, or the orphans at Penteli. It was my bed. In my room. A guest room, but my room just the same.

Agapi mou. My love. Her words slid along my newly cleaned body like warm water on icy skin. They melted away all the fears, the pain, the losses of the past two years, filling me with an awakening, a yearning for a different life, a different mother. One who shelters her children from harm instead of placing them at the center of a tornado's eye.

"You've seen too much." She tucked my hair behind my ears and kissed my forehead. Pity warmed her eyes and caressed the heaviness in me until I fell asleep, light and unencumbered. "Try to forget it all. You're safe now."

And I was. Safe. For the first time since our father left us to the precarious maelstroms that accompanied my mother's choices—whether they were her own or chosen for her. I will never know how much say she had in how it all unfolded for her. I don't see her having a lot of power, especially once Kristos came into her life.

Unlike my father, Kristos was brutal, violent. He found the weakest fish in the pond and consumed them. We never saw him coming. Or at least, I didn't. How could I? I only knew my father and my uncle George, the kind one who lived next door and lovingly cared for his girls.

Kristos was the first monster I found in men. My mother's johns, an array of them, followed. He opened the door for them and let them enter, for a price.

My uncle Dimitri, the uncle who took me into his family and home for a year, was also kind. But not present. I don't recall him as much as I do his wife, my aunt Efthalia. I remember going to the construction site he owned and managed during lunch, as my aunt and I brought him food and sat with him while he ate. I don't recall what he looked like or any words between us. He was quiet. He took me in, yes, but that was all.

It was my aunt who oversaw me. She was the one who held my hand and revived my heart, made me believe I was worth loving. She loved me. For a while. And that was everything to a little waif with nothing in her possession but a lot of love and forgiveness to dole out to anyone who would take a chance on her.

There were good men in my childhood, just not anyone who stayed or stood out. The good men were silent, ghosts who flitted in and out without a care in the world. Their quiet, absent personalities made them weak to someone like me who yearned for one of them to fight for me, to seize me from the ugly parts of my mother's life and protect me from them. From her. The mad men, the angry ones, they stayed, their savagery sharp and clear. They pricked holes of distrust on my skin and burrowed beneath the surface to hide there until they wanted to come out again, to remind me of my place, my insignificance.

For that entire year, though, I was free of them. Aside from my uncle and my cousin, men were absent. I was safe. And I thrived in that safety.

My aunt made sure I went to school, and because I felt loved and cared for, I enjoyed my learning. I didn't want to throttle anyone while living with my aunt and her children, John and Maria. And I wasn't afraid that my uncle Dimitri, her husband and my mother's own brother, would sneak into my bed at night and toss his heavy body over mine.

There was no fear for a full year. No anger. Just envy and a bit of curiosity about how some kids grew up in families that collectively loved them, while other kids, like me, were born to mothers like Athanasia, mad, poisoned, and debased. I envied my cousins for their mother, their father, and the loving home they grew up in. A home without strife or corruption. Until I came along, at least.

I still recall the day John and Maria came home from school, sat on the living room couch, and learned I would live with them. They didn't like me. How could they? I encroached upon their life, a private haven that existed just for them. I was an outsider. An outcast, dirty, diluted with debasement, and incoherent with my longings. I took their mother away from them, as she spent her free time clothing me, feeding me, and trying to bathe away the remnants of sin and ache that still clung to me like a sickly stench no amount of soap could coax from me. It hung on my hair, my skin, my breath even, and every word I uttered reminded them I didn't belong.

John, being an older boy, ignored me. But Maria was my favorite. She was blonde and brown-eyed, like my aunt, and I wanted her to like me so much that I ingratiated myself to her. I gushed over her prettiness, followed her everywhere like a lovesick puppy needing validation and love. When her friends came over, I wanted to play with them, and Maria shut the door in my face and told me to go away. I cried, and often, her mother found me teary-eyed and abandoned. I don't remember talks between mother and daughter over me, but I am sure there were a few. I was a pain in the ass, and in the end, Maria had the last word as to my fate.

John and Maria made sure they brought me home from school each day, but I walked behind them like a mangy rat following the scent of chicken scraps. I spent the earlier part of that year waiting for no one. I was a street urchin, crossing boulevards and begging on corners for drachmas on my own, unsupervised. Trailing behind my older cousins, who made it clear they didn't want me around, made me feel inferior to them. Unwanted, even.

One day, I decided I would leave the schoolyard without them. They were busy talking and laughing with their friends while I sat on a curb waiting for them, so I rose to my feet and walked home on my own. My aunt was visibly irritated, but not with me. With her kids.

"I was safe, *Thia*," I offered. "I looked both ways and asked a woman I saw to cross the street with me." I didn't say what I was thinking. That I had crossed many intersections without help in the past. That I didn't need my cousins to walk me home, to walk ahead of me as if I didn't exist.

But it didn't help. When my cousins got home, I was sent to my room, and my aunt and uncle talked with their kids. A few months later, they put me up for adoption. Just like that.

"Our children had a hard time with you at our home. I put

you up for adoption because I thought it would be best for everyone," my aunt Efthalia confessed when I was thirty and returned to Greece to retrieve my roots before having children of my own. "I thought it would be best for you. If I had known how much it hurt you, I would have kept you."

How can I fault a mother who gives up that which is hurting her family's peace? I never did. I just wish there had been a mother out there who would have sacrificed for me. And now that I am fifty, motherless still, this is a wish I have to put aside, like a favorite childhood toy I am too old to play with.

My reprieve was momentary, a lapse in time that warranted a much-needed rest, but life went on. This family continued without me. And I embarked on a new journey. Without them. After all, I wasn't theirs. No matter how much I wanted to belong to them. To have a mother and a home just like theirs.

OKAY, BABA

I often wonder if my expectations of motherhood would not have been set so high for Ann if I had not spent a year with my aunt. Albeit brief, this encounter with the gentle maternal, the loving home and family she engendered, set me up for the next mother in my life. One better than the first, but in stark contrast to the mother of my longings, my aunt Efthalia. If I had not spent a year being loved and touched with appreciation by my aunt, I would not have believed that mothers could be like this.

Had I gone straight from the physical negligence of Athanasia to the emotional negligence of Ann, I would not have known any better. I would not have expected more. But my aunt did intercept — by the hand of God or the universe, whichever reigns over chance or fate. And my encounter with her changed me. Made me believe I was worth loving. Worthy of the mother I found in her. Ann had no chance of measuring up to the nurturing mother my aunt had been to me.

When I first met Ann, my family had already decided that she would become my mother. My fate was determined, even though no one had met her beforehand. Not my aunt Efthalia, who gave me to her. And not my father, who surprised me with a visit to my aunt's house after a three-year absence from my life.

I was seven the day I returned from school in Nea Smyrni to find him in my aunt's kitchen, waiting for me. Still hurt by his earlier rejection of me, I couldn't find any words to offer him. A thick wad of saliva collected inside my cheeks and sealed my mouth, gluing my lips together. I sat in the chair opposite him, my heart smashing against my chest with the ferocity of a ship caught in a maelstrom.

"How are you, Marinoula mou?" My eyes blinked at the endearment. *Marinoula mou.* My little Marina. I was his. But was I? The last words he had spoken to me three years earlier were a denial of me. They implied I was a bastard, even though I looked like him with my deep brown eyes, my olive skin, and the blondish-brown hair both my brothers and I shared with him.

"*Kala,*" I said. Fine. Good. Was he here to take me back? To reclaim me? I held my breath.

"I thought we could spend some time together. You can spend the night with me when I pick you up from here every Saturday. I'm living with my sister, Georgia. Do you remember her?" He paused for my answer.

I nodded my head. I remember her hiding around the corner of our house, trying to catch my mother abusing her brother, so she could finally have proof, a reason to take him away. To care for him. To leave his kids behind, unprotected.

"Do you want to go with me tonight?"

I nodded my head. What was I supposed to say? No? I was seven. He came back for me. I was too young to think of anything else, for any reason other than that he wanted me back. Maybe we could get my brothers, too. And Maria. And Eleni. And we could be a family again.

For the next two weeks, my father picked me up on Saturdays, took me to his sister's home, and then returned me the following day. The days spent with my father were quiet, warm.

I didn't have a voice yet—not an external one—not the kind that my daughter, Rena, has at fifteen. She would have looked at him, twisted her mouth into a smirk, and said aloud, "What the fuck, Dad? What is wrong with you?" I was not that kind of child. I was not given that kind of social power in my family.

I was a stranger, treated like one, like a burden passed from one hand to the next as if I were too much trouble to handle. And I felt like trouble, the kind of trouble I was relieved to know people were trying to take care of, even if it meant putting me on a plane and sending me off to a complete and utter stranger in a foreign land.

I have internalized this victimhood status, this problematic character as an adult. I don't bother my friends with my troubles, and when I feel as if my problems are too much for them, I curl into silence and bear it on my own because I don't want to feel like a burden. Again. They might give me away. Stop taking my calls. Pass me off to another stranger. Abandon me. The way my father did. My mother. My aunt. Eventually, Ann. And even Richard.

It only took two visits before my father sat me down at the kitchen table, with my aunt Efthalia and uncle Dimitri a few feet away, to explain to me his sudden return.

"We found a wonderful woman to adopt you," he told me. Not quite in those words. I don't remember the exact words. But it was something akin to this. "She is American and lives in New York. She's a teacher. A science teacher, and she wants you to be her daughter." I said nothing. I just looked at him, trying to understand why he had come back just to send me away again.

"We will always be your family, but this is the best thing for you," my aunt Efthalia interjected from behind me. I didn't turn around to look at her. I only felt my shoulders sink with the weight of understanding. He didn't want me. But she didn't want me, either. Not even after a year of keeping me. I was that unlovable. Unkeepable.

"Okay, Baba." I nodded my head in agreement, as if I had a say.

"Okay, *Thia*," I told my aunt as she helped me pack my things.

"Okay, Mama," I told my mother, Athanasia, when she called to tell me goodbye.

"Okay, Baba," I smiled when my father spent the last day with me by taking me to see Stavros and Nikos and Maria at their respective orphanages. Stavros and Nikos pushed me on the swings, laughing aloud as if it weren't the end. As if we were happy. Nikos hung upside down on the monkey bars and scratched his armpits, making ape sounds until I laughed.

With Maria, at a different orphanage for girls on the other side of the city, it was different. Somber. She was lying in bed and ill. There was no laughter, no smile. I sat by her bedside in silence and watched her. I don't remember any words between us and won't pretend there were any. I kissed her cheek when my dad pulled me away to leave, and I haven't seen her since. Not even when I returned to Greece. She's the only sibling I cannot locate. She has disappeared.

"Okay, Baba," I'm sure was the last phrase I said to my father when he dropped me off at my aunt's house for the last time. Why would I say anything different? I know I pretended to be happy to be given away as much as they pretended to be happy to give me away. I was a pleaser even back then, hoping that by being amenable, forgiving, someone would love me enough to keep me.

I use this term, *give me away*, because that is exactly what it was. I was a thing. Given away. To a stranger. Not quite an orphan because orphans don't have parents and relatives. But I had all of those. I had a father and a mother and siblings and a shitload of aunts, uncles, and cousins. A lot of them. And yet, I had no one. No one to stand up for me. To grab me, pull me to their hip like they do in movies and say, "You are mine. I will die before someone takes you from me."

How hard is it to want a child? To love a child? To make a child *feel* loved and wanted? It's not difficult for me. And yet, I was surrounded by a slew of people who didn't want me. Didn't love me. It had to be me. Something about me, right?

That feeling never goes away. It's a rabid dog that sleeps beside you each night, drooling on your corner of the pillow, a constant reminder of your worthlessness that makes you wonder why you go on.

Nothing fills the emptiness.

I know. I've tried.

There's an unfathomable hole in me, and everything I fill it with just seeps right back out, leaving me empty again. There's only one relief I know will help for good, and I struggle to stay away from it. It is a siren's call, filling me with images of slitting my wrists, playfully seducing the hardness of life out of me, out of my body, a body that has endured abuse and neglect and bloodied losses—and now just wants to sleep. To rest. To die, even.

But I stay, and I say, "Okay."

"Okay, new mother. Lead the way," I told Ann, accepting her without resistance.

"You were always a people pleaser," Ann told me years ago when she described me as a child. She pursed her lips and raised her eyebrows the way she did whenever she wanted to show me her displeasure. Pleasing people wasn't a gift, a sign of moral character. It was a sign of weakness. I spent my childhood bending myself to please her, distorting and silencing myself to make her love me, but it didn't matter.

Nothing I did endeared me to her. I was a damaged, broken, and unfixable child as soon as I set foot in her American home and wept for my father. That's all it took to displease her and no number of cards or poems or self-erasure designed to prove my loyalty and love made her believe I was meant to be hers and hers alone.

Of course, she had not met me yet. Only the promise of me. My family showed her the only picture they had of me at the time, a passport picture, black and white, with chopped up brown hair and uneven bangs. I was small and cute and mute in that picture, and Ann believed I would answer her call and fill the holes inside her, without being told about all the holes in me she would need to fill—and chose not to. She adopted me for her, not for me.

Mine was a "word-of-mouth" adoption. Ann's aunt Maria lived a few blocks from my aunt Efthalia's home in Nea Smyrni. She let it be known that her Greek American niece wanted to adopt a Greek girl, and my aunt heard and responded to the call: *Yes, we have one to give away.* Minus the sarcasm, I suppose. That's my own to add, because it all occurred without an official meeting taking place. And without my knowledge.

No one met Ann. No one met her aunt Maria. It was just decided. My father told me it would happen, and one day, a social worker by the name of Mrs. Pappas came into my aunt Efthalia's home, packed me up, and swept me away like a used, unwanted toy my cousins were too old to play with. A taxicab took us twenty minutes away to an apartment building in the same part of town in Athens, and deposited me into the home of my new mother's aunt. I lived with her for one year while the adoption was finalized, and I didn't see my father, my mother, my aunt, or my siblings again.

Not until I turned thirty. And by that time, I was different. English had replaced my Greek. Ann forbade me from sharing my memories because she didn't believe them, or me, and I reimagined all my longings for love and acceptance onto a woman who had possession of me for twenty-plus years and would not love me.

But until I knew the truth—that all this, my father's return, was a ruse to set me up for giving me away to a stranger and my aunt's refusal to keep me in her home and family—I loved every moment I spent with my father. He took me on long walks in the evenings, and even though we didn't say more than two words to each other, I bumped against his arm just to feel his hands on me. I inched closer to him for a brief whiff of the smoke that he exhaled into the moist summer air, mingled with his breath, a combination of garlic and onions from his sister's *horiatiki* salad with hearty tomatoes and feta cheese cubes mixed with olive oil, oregano, and red onions. He took me to the local taverna and bought me lamb souvlaki with a piece of warm bread staked on the sharp tip of the stick. I gulped a sip of Coke from my bottle and bit off a piece of the lamb, feeling full on the inside and warm on the outside.

It's all a little girl like me needed. Food, drink, and her baba. I just wanted to be his. To know I was his. To walk beside him, taking bites of the meal he bought for me, mesmerized by the motion of his feet as they moved in harmony with mine, the sharp blue tint of television sets peeking from windows along the homes we passed during our stroll around the neighborhood.

Even today, without him beside me, without the souvlaki, I smile every time I see the blue tint of television sets flashing from apartment windows or homes when I walk in the evenings. I am fifty, have been fatherless almost all my life, and yet he always comes back to me with every blue television light and every evening walk I take. As if he were with me still. As if he had left the gentlest part of my childhood with me. The quietest, sweetest parts of him to look after.

Even afterward, when he took me back to my aunt's and told me the truth, why he had come back. Even now. Now that I know clearly why he returned, I still hold onto those moments — the walks, the blue lights, the souvlaki kabobs, the silences between us—and I love him for giving them to me. I can't hate him. I won't. It's over. He's dead. What's done is done.

He was a survivor, and he did what he needed to survive.

I'm a survivor, too, and I have walked away from those who hurt me—my adoptive mother, my husband—because they could. I can't hate my father because I am him, albeit a better, stronger version. I didn't abandon my kids. But I'm also a woman. Born of violence, raised in debasement, struggling still to plant my feet on soil that may prove to be another sinkhole, another disappointment.

Unlike my father, and perhaps because I am a woman, a mother unlike the two mothers who raised me, I take my kids with me, planting one foot in front of the other to show them what it looks like to survive, to stay, to love hard and true, without tricks or manipulating lies, and to live in a life that is so damn hard to enjoy—but to live it, anyway. Because I am a woman, a mother, and I do it for my kids—for the joy I find only in their smiles, in the light they bring to some very hard and very dark days that just never seem to end.

It is not an exaggeration to say that I live for my kids. That I stay here, among the debris and dregs of a life and people that have never brought me much pleasure, never made me feel safe or wanted or loved—that I stay here for them. For Joseph and Rena. They are the only ones I believe in. The only ones I love. The only glimmers of hope I keep close to my chest. To remind my heart to keep beating despite my unwillingness.

THE ORPHANAGE

*A*lthough I don't remember being sexually abused, my body has always reminded me I was in the way I respond to my children's touches. Like most PTSD memories, many of them coexist with me, breathing beneath relative blackness, like ghosts who only come out when triggered, forced by a séance that refuses to let them rest in peace. It is in the mothering of my children, however, that I have become most aware of the hurts in my body, the aging, creaking bones, resisting touch, my skin growing cold, my body turning to stone.

Sometimes, my children's touches fill me with consternation. It's an odd and unforgiving thing to say, but my body bends with inexplicable discomfort from past hurts I barely recall. Because I don't remember them, I don't understand my reactions. And I can't name them for my children or take away the hurt expressions that linger in their eyes when I jerk my arm away suddenly or shift my hips to place some distance between us.

My visceral responses to touch are more obvious because of my daughter, Rena. I don't remember jerking myself away when my son was little. Joseph wasn't as touch-heavy or touch-persistent as she has been. My son is a bit more like me—observing quietly, taking only when it's given, whatever the "it" is—love, hugs, conversation, food. Even now, at nineteen, I must remind him he needs to eat, to shower. That he needs to be touched, to have his skin caressed, his hair tousled, his body curved into mine for daily doses of sustenance. If I don't go to him to give him these basic needs, he won't seek them out. He'll go days without, as I often did, and he won't ask for what he needs. He doesn't know he needs it until it is offered to him. I know because this is how I am.

But my daughter, at fifteen, is quite different. Rena has always sought me out. To play with her, to hug her, to lie down with her until she is confident the moths or gnats or mosquitoes having found refuge in her room have flown out of it, and she can sleep peacefully. While my son seems to have perceived my physical discomforts with touch and respected them, my daughter rejects the possibility that her mother's body may have corners and edges that feel a lot like dragging one's nails across a chalkboard when touched.

"Stop manhandling me," I joke with her when she wraps her arms around my neck to keep me from moving away from her closeness—a closeness I love and climb into but need to move out of when it gets to be too long and my limbs feel like they can't breathe, suffocating in a smoke fire, too polite to move out of the way. I untangle the roots of her arms slowly from around my waist, with practiced maneuvering and laughter spewing from my lips, kissing her face and hair and fingertips so she can't read the distress behind my movements.

"Your elbow is digging into my thigh," I warn her when she climbs on top of me, her long, lithe body, now two inches longer than my five-foot-one-and-shrinking form. I try not to push her away from me, aware of the tenderness in her, the need she has to touch me—to force touch into me.

"I can't be touched here or there," I tell her, pointing to the bones protruding from my ankles and clavicles and hips and kneecaps and elbows. "I can't feel like I am being bolted down, forced," I explain to her when she tries to trap my arms above my head.

"You can't play with me the way you play with your dad," I remind her. When she and Richard play, they wrestle, and he lets her throw karate kicks at him or punch him in the gut—because he's fast and can outmaneuver her. It's a game between them. But it's hard to explain to her that I don't play this way. I don't play at all. I can't. If I get kicked or hit on the head, even accidentally, it all goes dark behind my eyes.

"Why do you have all these weird reactions?" Rena asks after I remind her not to touch my knee, that it grates on my nerves, that my entire body bends into itself like a magnet being pulled to the center of its force.

"I don't know." I shake my head at her. "Something to do with my childhood, I suppose."

"You don't remember?" She sits on the floor beside my bed, folding our fluffy cat into her arms. The cat doesn't recoil, doesn't object. She nestles against my daughter's chest like she belongs there.

I remember some, I want to say to her, but I don't. She's too young yet to know everything about me. About the dark places, the abysmal cliffs that lead to even more blackness.

"Not really," I say. "I just know it feels like my bones go rigid and want to push their way through my skin."

"That's weird," she says, looking at me with a thoughtful gaze that tells me she'll be okay—despite me.

"Yes. It is." I lean over and kiss her on the cheeks and forehead and hair. All the places I know she loves, trying to remove the stains of rejection I keep leaving behind.

What I don't share with her is the period in my childhood when I was taken away from my birth mother and put in an orphanage for girls in the epicenter of Athens. Penteli was its name. The funny thing about this orphanage is I never quite felt like I belonged there. After all, orphans don't have a family. I did. But I ended up there anyway, because when they found me, I was alone.

My hazy memories estimate I spent a year there and was around five years old when someone — let's say the police — found me playing alone in a sandbox at the park. My mother was nowhere to be found, which meant she had stepped away for a bit with a john, behind the trees or into the bathroom or in his car, leaving me in the park to wait for her. She left me there often, and then returned, arranging herself on the park bench so that her skirt hiked up along her creamy white thigh, an invitation for more johns to taste and pay.

I know she hadn't placed me at the orphanage because during my first night at Penteli, she came for me, pounding her fists against the heavy wooden doors, screaming my name into the hallway when the nuns finally opened them.

"Marina! *Pou eisai. Ella etho!*" I heard my name, her voice calling to me, demanding I run to her, but I refused to go. I saw this for what it was. An opportunity to escape my mother's prostitution and Kristos's ever-growing fascination with me.

I buried myself deeper under the crisp, clean covers of my new bed instead, hoping the nuns would make her go away. Where would I go back to if they returned me to her? Not to a warm bed or a safe home. It would have been back to the streets for me. Back to watching her sell herself, or having sex with Kristos in front of me, or dragging Eleni and her sticky, suckled fingers from one corner to the next, picking her up and carrying her when she was too tired, hungry, and hot to walk or run or sit still. The worst part though was sleeping on hard, cold floors in buildings on construction sites, my recollections of sleeping in the warmth of our old house faint but ever-present.

None of me wanted to go back to any of it.

Beneath my covers, I prayed to the God the Penteli nuns told me was watching out for me to keep me safe from her and Kristos. Eventually, the pounding stopped, and the nuns explained to her she would have to come back the next day to see me.

She did. Athanasia returned with my little sister riding on her hip. And with Kristos.

"You must stay here," she explained to me at the picnic table by the playground. With arms folded against my chest and chin tucked into my neck, my eyes traced every movement Kristos made as he paced back and forth in the background, telling her to hurry: *"Ella, mana mou."*

Let's go, my woman. *My* woman. Such possession. Such ownership. I wanted to lunge at him the way I did in my dreams and throw a series of punches in his face, erasing the cocky grin he planted there like a recurring weed just to taunt me.

"I'll come back for you," I heard her say from the guarded haze of my memories. "I have to get a place for us, an apartment, and then they will let me take you back."

I didn't say anything. Words weren't in my arsenal as a child. I was often mute but watchful, angry, and stubborn in the memories I hold of myself as a little girl. I observed, I took notes, and I collected words and faces and memories as if I knew I would need them one day to excavate and dissect the damage she and Kristos would leave behind in me.

"Give your baba a kiss," she bid me as they readied to leave the orphanage.

"Then eine o babas mou!"

He's not my daddy, I seethed at her, my chest and mouth full of unrelenting hurt. I turned and ran in the opposite direction, toward Penteli and its Greek Orthodox nuns. Without my mother, Eleni, or Kristos.

Kristos was not my father. I did not belong to him. And for the next year, I didn't belong to anyone. I was a waif. A ward of the state. An orphan.

I didn't like Penteli, but a stalwart building with four walls, rooms with doors, nested with girls and black-clad nuns was better than what my mother offered me. She left me there because she had no choice; the state refused to surrender me to her until she had an apartment and could provide me with four walls, a ceiling, an address, and food in the refrigerator.

I have strong memories of resistance at Penteli, and they flood me with images of an enraged child held together by stiff shoulders and a proud chin, arms pinned to my chest, a scowling expression stitched across my mouth like a battle scar one refused to remove.

Was I angry because the nuns were harsh and hit us? Or because I wanted to be with my mother even though life with her was harrowing in its unpredictability? Or was it because I was abused there?

I don't know the truth behind the rage that coursed through me like ice, thick and solid enough to make me stand so straight someone could easily snap me in two with their fingertips, like a crisp string bean.

During the reunion in my thirties, I asked my family if Kristos had abused me.

"No, no!" They shook their heads with such vehemence I almost believed them. But how would they know? They weren't there. I was. Eleni was. My mother and Kristos were.

No one will tell the truth, not even my memories, with only my body crying out for help, the nerve endings grinding against each other like a warbled shriek waking me up in the middle of the night. So why can no one touch me? Why do I cringe at the slightest touch as if I am on fire? Why can't I get a massage or slip into a hug or be loved physically?

Kristos threatened to teach me about sex, to make me like my mother. If I had stayed with them, they would have taught me to use my sex for money. I watched him have sex with my mother, slept on the same mattress with them, their naked bodies crammed against my smaller, fully clothed one. He kissed me on the lips, grabbing my face with both hands until I relented, shutting my eyes and allowing his mouth and smell to leave stains on me.

"Kristos used to slam his boombox against your head," Eleni reminded me during our reunion in 1999.

"Why did he do that?" I laughed at the idea of someone hitting me. It makes sense why getting hit accidentally sends me into a whirlwind of emotions—anger, really. Rage, more like it.

"You were counter-reactive." She smiled at me. "You didn't take his shit and talked back to him whenever he told you what to do."

"How old was I then? Five? Six?"

She nodded and smiled.

Where is that girl? Fighting back. Rude. Belligerent. I don't know her anymore. I am polite now. Quiet. A body of surrenders.

"They abused us at the orphanage," my brother Stavros told me, watching me from behind the cloud of cigarette smoke billowing about his features. Dark eyes, grim mouth. He didn't like talking about our childhood, but he understood I had come to them with questions.

My siblings contained the roots of their memories and lived on with our family, examining them through the recollections of every living member. They had these talks before. I was the missing link. I had traveled across the world, with no one to talk to me about them, no one to tell me what they remembered of me as a child, to help me piece together the quilt of fragmented images Ann forbade me to talk about in my new life away from them.

"Nikos and I, we were abused by the other boys in the orphanage." His tone was quiet, matter of fact. "Sexually," he added, in case I hadn't understood. "It's why Nikos is the way he is. I managed it somehow, but all of it affected Nikos."

"What happened to him?" I hadn't met him yet. We were in Athens, and he lived in Crete. He couldn't travel, so I didn't meet him until my second trip to Greece the following year, which took me first to Athens to collect Eleni and then to Crete to visit

Stavros and meet my other brother, Nikos, the second-born of the Koutrogiannis children.

"He drinks most of the day and night. He is homeless. He has seizures, too, and I take care of him when I can. I take him food and clothes. But he's volatile. He blows up, cries, sleeps, and drinks away his life." Stavros took a long drag from his cigarette and blew out the smoke before continuing. "I try to help him, but he's difficult. He's not all there all the time. He lives a lot in his childhood, and the more he talks about it, the angrier he gets."

I nodded my head, waiting for him to continue, not wanting to force the conversation, but he didn't. He had said all he wanted to say.

"Yes," Eleni's voice filled in the pause. "It happened to me, too, when I was in the orphanage for girls. It's very common."

"I remember some things from Penteli," I told them. "But I've blocked much of it." *And I was there for only a year, maybe less*, I wanted to add but knew better. They had spent their entire childhood there, not being released until they were eighteen years old. I didn't want to remind them, yet again, how I had escaped that life sentence, that kind of neglect.

The abuse my brothers suffered was so severe, they later told me, that Stavros and Nikos ran away from the orphanage and went to the local newspaper to tell them what happened. Instead of writing an exposé on the sexual and physical abuses at the orphanage, they sent for the police, who put them in a car and kept them for the night in a holding cell. When my brothers woke up, they were in Crete, in a completely different orphanage for boys, a plane ride away from the city of Athens.

My memories of Penteli come and go, but they're always the same. My arms crossed about my chest, visibly pissed off. Failing first grade because I refused to do any work. My mother visiting me with Kristos and my little sister, Eleni. Leaving me there, promising to return for me once she secured an apartment. Then later the same day, eating peas during dinner and vomiting them all back up again, the nuns rushing toward me and picking up the pieces my mother left behind.

I remember lying in my bed at night, pretending to sleep, when the older girls came and blew a puff of air across my closed lids. I was afraid of them, held my breath, and snapped my eyes shut, willing them not to flutter. It's as if I knew what would happen if they caught me with my eyes open. But how did I know? Had I seen something? Like many of my memories from this time, there were no linear images telling me the full narrative. There was no exposition, no climax, no resolution. There was just the moment and all the trepidation that came with it, like a bullet lodged in my bones, corroding my insides.

I don't know what happened afterward. I have one sharp memory of clamping my eyes shut and holding my breath while an older girl bent over me, blowing her breath against my lids, and then opening them to see if she was gone. But she wasn't. The browns of our eyes clashed, and her lips slid into a sinister smile. I don't remember much else.

I know something happened because, eventually, by the time I left Penteli, I was having sex with other girls. I had been taught— forced or otherwise—about kissing and touching and rubbing my parts against another girl's pubic bones in the middle of the night. I was aware of the older girls recruiting the newest ones in the dark, our guardian-nuns asleep in private rooms away from the main hall in which our iron-cast beds sat side-by-side and row by row.

In one of my memories, another little girl and I pulled our cots together after the nuns went to bed and turned off the lights, burrowed under the covers, took our clothes off, and kissed, our flat, prepubescent chests and hairless hips smashing into each other in the hopes the friction engendered would feed us the intimacy and touch and love we had been deprived of by our parents and the nuns who grew us like weeds on unkempt lawns.

A year later, when I was living with my aunt and uncle, I found myself in a camp for girls. The only moment I have held onto from this camp and this one summer was a rendezvous in the woods with another girl my age. We played house, but I was the man who came home from work and expected dinner at the table, a stump of a tree sitting between us. She was my wife, I was her husband, and when I pulled her to me, she succumbed to my kisses. She was pliable and soft and kissed me back. We lay naked on the dirt floor of our natural home, playing with each other's hair, laughing into the breeze, goosebumps rushing to the surface of our young, aching flesh.

Maybe there was no abuse, no rape, no tying me down with force. Or maybe there was. I don't remember how the hard parts of my childhood began. I only remember the in-betweens, like the soft, sweet middle of Oreo cookies, smooth and satisfying as it slides down my throat and sinks in my belly. I only recall the digestible parts, the palatable ones. My body tells me otherwise, but there is no evidence, no verbal or physical corroboration. It's an "it said/she said" scenario where my body screams that something happened to her, but the world around me demands proof. Bruises. A recording. A time and a place. A name, even. A witness.

But I have no proof. No witnesses. Only a collection of loose memories I stitched together with untrained fingers and the way my body feels in me, like it doesn't belong. Like it wants to climb out of me and run away, put a knife to its throat and end the catastrophe that riddles it.

"You've seen terrible things," my aunt Efthalia once told me right before my adoption, when my memories were still fresh. She believed me because she knew my mother, knew where I had come from. "Try to forget it, my love. You will be going to America soon, and you will have a new mother and a new life. It's the best thing for you."

"Don't lie to me," Ann told me a year later when the memories were still raw. I was eight, trying to confess the sins creeping along my flesh like fleas in search of root—so she would know me, know where I had come from, and love me anyway. It never occurred to me she wouldn't believe me. But she didn't. And this disbelief in my nature, my truth, laid out the fragile foundation of all our arguments and disagreements, a mother–daughter conflict that persists today.

"I won't tolerate liars in my home." She rose from the kitchen table and left me there, quiet and still. I was aware for the first time that my childhood was intolerable, a thing of shame and disgust I shouldn't talk about. Not to her. Not to anyone.

When she took away my name and renamed me Kathryn, after her mother, I understood that Marina and her memories could no longer exist in me. Ann wanted a daughter without ties to my past, as if I were an infant she had pushed out of her unused womb, my bloody pulp cradled in her arms. I had a new home, country, and life. I had a new mother. A new identity. And in this life, I was expected to cast away my experiences and build new ones to replace them. Anything else was unacceptable.

So I made myself from scratch, and my early losses remained unvoiced and unfed, like orphans locked away in the cellar, in the dark, with no chinks of light to promise them a way out, until one by one, they self-aborted, ripped from my own battered uterus and thrown in the trash, where they writhed and gasped for one more breath, one more utterance to remind me they existed. That I existed, too, as Marina, before Kathryn took over the weight I had once known as belonging only to me.

PART II

Ann, The Asexual Mother, The Virgin

HOW TO ERASE
A STRONG GIRL

My second mother, Ann, adopted me when I was eight. She was the polar opposite of my birth mother. She was contained, in control, and asexual. In all the years I lived with her, until my twenty-fifth birthday, she never dated. Men were absent from her life, and despite my unhappiness, it seemed like fate had assigned me to a new mother who lived on her own terms, without relying on men for food or home or love.

"I don't need a man," she often told me. She didn't. She only called on men for help when she needed a plumber or a mechanic. And she paid them for their service. With money, not sex.

She'd received proposals from men when she was younger, she told me, but she was not interested. They were Greek men, and although she herself was Greek, she thought they were all "peasants." She was too educated for them, too smart, too evolved. She was independent, made her own rules, owned her own properties—a summer house in Stonybrook and a three-story apartment building in Queens—and built her own career. There was nothing a man could give her that she hadn't already given herself.

What about love? I often wanted to ask her but couldn't. We didn't have that kind of relationship. She was the authority. I was the ungrateful adopted child. We were never friends. Never soft with each other. Or open. Or loving.

Love would have softened her up, but that is why she adopted me, no? I was supposed to bring her the love she'd lost

when her parents died. The love she denied me when she realized I was just as hungry for love as she was. We were both
running on empty, like two vampires scratching and clawing
our way through mounds of bodies in search of one drop of
what we had been denied.

I wanted her love; she wanted mine. But neither one of us
had the tools we needed to extract it from the other. So we went
hungry, digging our fingers through the lint in our belly buttons,
trying to retrieve the umbilical cord that had once connected us
to a mother's womb for the nourishment we needed and expected
in our pairing.

Through her, though, I learned what a body looks like when
it respects itself—or when its occupant respects herself and her
body. She was in charge of her own money, unlike the first mother
I knew, whose money was controlled by a man. As was her body.

Ann was forty-eight when she adopted me, and she taught
me that the mind was the most important part of a woman. Not
through words. We never really said much to each other. But
through her actions. I watched, and I took notes, wanting to emulate her not only for my survival as a girl with sex-stained roots
but also for her love. If I were like her, then maybe she would
love me, too, the way she loved herself.

A high school science teacher, she owned her own three-story
building and rented out the two apartments below hers. She was
a landlady. She drove her own car, a military-green Chevy Nova
that stalled every time it rained or snowed. I spent many hours of
my childhood sitting in the back, and later, when I was older, in
the front, rolling my eyes as she turned the key in the ignition
again and again in the hopes the car would start, impatient New
Yorkers sounding their horns at us on the highway. But my
mother was frugal and purchased a new car only when the Nova
died of old age and was too costly to bring back to life.

Ann was all about using her intelligence, feeding her brain, collecting degrees, and advancing her position in life. She went to night school and weekend school, graduating with a master's degree not only in secondary education but also in library science. By the time I was in college, she had transitioned from classroom science teacher to school librarian.

I was in awe of Ann. I spent my entire childhood looking up to her, worshipping her, her eyes returning my gaze with debasement. I was a peasant, a Greek from Greece. She hated them. She was different. Her family was from Turkey. Turkish Greeks were a better sort of Greek than the Greek Greeks I came from.

"Greeks from Greece are peasants. Users. Phony," she tells me this still, at ninety to my fifty, arching her eyebrows at me as if to say, *that includes you.*

"I'm Greek. From Greece," I remind her now that I am older and bolder. Not because she forgets, but because I grow tired of being insulted by her, pretending her words don't cling to my skin like sharp claws.

But as a child, I had no voice. Fear of displeasing her eroded my spirit, the enamel on my teeth when they clenched against my gums to force my mouth shut lest I show my true Greek roots. Fear that she, too, would abandon me. I was in a foreign country with a foreign tongue, and a foreign woman with a foreign way of communicating, her long drawn-out silences and piercing eyes rendering me an erased and alien thing.

I lived in my body in those days, the only comfortable suitcase I could find to fold myself into. I fit into it perfectly, silence humming between us, drowning out the emotional tremors that came with abandonment, with living with a stranger I didn't know how to please. My body was my only friend then, comforting me, enveloping me, teaching me how to brace myself whenever Ann glared at me with such disappointment it felt like the slaps I had once endured from Kristos, the crusted skin of his fingers leaving red marks on my cheek.

As much as Athanasia taught me to detach myself from my body and my sex, to fear them, Ann taught me to loathe my body, to see it and its needs as shameful. I suppose because that is how she saw my body, how she saw me. I was a danger because I came from illicit roots, tangled, not amenable to the prim and proper gardens she cultivated in her own backyard.

The only true thing she knew about my years before her was that my mother was a "whore." It's the only fact my social worker told her, that and that I was in an orphanage, plagued by marasmus, the wasting away of the flesh.

When I acted out by going roller-skating with my friends against her wishes when I was eleven or having a friend over to the house when I was thirteen or going over to my friend's house down the block to watch Disney movies when I was twenty-one, Ann called me a whore.

Putana is the Greek version of the word. She knew very little about my childhood, never asked me about it, and didn't find it necessary to ask the social worker on my case for more details. But she knew my mother was a whore. It was true in her mind that I would also become one. Even though I was a virgin until the age of twenty-five, I was still a whore in her eyes.

Ann's fear was that I would disgrace her. Her cousin had warned her against adopting me, an older child from unknown roots, she told me later, when I was in my twenties. Another distant cousin, she told me, adopted two older girls, and they had run away, turning to the streets, selling their bodies for survival. A cautionary tale against adopting older children, girls in particular, since we bear shame in our sex and our bodies. Because I was older when she adopted me, I was a threat. Complicit, even.

A woman who lived her life in control, with no one at the helm of her one-woman existence, the last thing Ann needed was a child composed of everything she couldn't control. She never really understood that someone like me, a child coming from the dregs of society where control was not part of her experience and chaos was an everyday occurrence, would thrill at being surrounded by adults who controlled themselves, their bodies, and the scariest part of human existence to me, their sexuality.

Of course, all these fears, mine and hers, didn't show up until a year into my adoption. None of this information was available to us when we first met.

When we first met, I was seven. A quiet child, I resolved that Ann would be my new mom without resistance. My father told me this would be a better life for me, and I had no choice but to believe him.

I mean, I couldn't really protest, could I?

I swallowed the news of adoption and abandonment with the adaptive skills of a kid who had spent the past three years being shuffled from one home to the next, from one moment of relief to more chaos.

Ann was my last chance. My only chance. If she didn't like me, who would? Where would I go? Where else could they put me? Back with my birth mother? Back at the orphanage? Ann was the better choice, wasn't she?

So I smiled at her, enchanted by the brown and green jagged gems that adorned her elegant fingers, her palms lovely and warm, promising a gentleness I expected would persist.

Ann spoke to me in Greek, her accent strong and foreign. She was Greek, yes, born in Greece, but she had grown up in the United States and spoke that language in such a way that no one could tell it was her second tongue. I smiled at the awkward phrases she uttered in Greek and couldn't wait to learn English, because that would endear me to her, bond us so that language would not act as a barrier to our love.

I loved her then. I didn't need much to love an adult at seven. Just a slip of a kind word, a gentle reminder to hold my fork the right way, to chew with my mouth closed, and the promise to teach me how to sew my dresses on her Singer sewing machine once I arrived in New York, where she lived. That's all it took for a desperate girl like me.

She was a promise. Hope. She was everything and everyone I hadn't known but knew existed. Everything and everyone I thought I deserved, finally, despite the bedraggled roots still attached to my ankles.

When I discovered she had two moles on the same parts of her body as I did, one above her left breast and one below her shoulder blades, I told myself that she was God's design. He had created her for me. A woman, alone, seeking a little girl to raise. To protect. To love. The twin moles were points on a road map so we could find each other. And we did. I was happy and charmed by her, so much so that I charmed her into believing it was the same with me. I was nice and sweet and polite and quiet. On my best behavior. My most perfect self, the self that she would adore and not want to part with. Ever.

She blamed me later, in my teen years. Blamed me for tricking her into adopting me. Tricking her into believing I was a good, obedient child. She didn't tell me directly, but it is how I understood the sly comments she tossed in my direction when she found me displeasing.

"You're such an ingrate. I've sacrificed for you, and this is how you repay me," is one.

"You were difficult as a child," is another. "You did everything you could to manipulate those around you. Even your teachers noticed."

"Kathryn is using you," she told a few of my friends, calling them without my knowledge in elementary school, middle school, and college. "Don't be friends with her. Don't trust her. You're just a pawn in her game, and she's using you to get her way." This was a recurring one, being uttered to my childhood friend Joyce as early as sixth grade. I was only eleven, had been her daughter for all of three years, but as early as that, she determined that I had tricked her into adopting me.

"I'm thinking of adopting another girl. A Chinese girl," she told me one day. I was twelve, passing her in the hallway on my way to the kitchen. Like sharp nails hammered against the back of my head, those words still grind into me, rotted and rusted.

"Do whatever you want," I mumbled and continued to walk past her, turning my head so she wouldn't catch the red humiliation in my eyes, or the tears that were ready to twist out of me with an ache I couldn't understand. Asian children were my mother's favorite students. They were smart, quiet, submissive, and often gravitated to musical skills I did not have. Ten years of violin lessons did not induce her to love me. I didn't play well enough. I wasn't becoming a skilled musician, which had been her original wish for me. But I hated the violin because she forced it on me, because every time she made me audition for music schools and private teachers, I wasn't good enough to be accepted, and I failed her. Again and again, in every way.

To make things worse, I was Greek. From Greece. A peasant. I was not the girl I pretended to be when she'd found me adorable and sweet in her aunt's apartment in Athens during the adoption process. I was wild. A whore in the making. A failure in obedience and gratitude because I kept asking for more. For love. For more than she had in her teacup to pour into my empty pitcher.

Although Ann's skin was soft, frail even, she was capable of coldness, a severing that made me feel like an extra limb she decided was unnecessary to her livelihood. She could go months pretending I didn't exist even though I was living in a room in her house, another body haunting the hallway corridors she owned. I screamed and pulled out my hair and crashed my bookcase against the wall of my room, my books toppling onto my head, just to prove to her I was there, I was hers, but each time, she stood still, quiet, unmoved by my passions and frustrations. She didn't see my pain. She only saw her own. She only saw my wickedness, my lack of self-control.

But I was good. A good girl. A loving, hopeful girl, despite all the failed attempts at love that had been promised me—and were easily revoked. My rebellions came out in words—in the insistence that I was worthy. Even back then, as a child, I believed myself worthy of love—her love. I was who I promised her I would be. I did well in school. I learned English in two years and read books as if English words had been born in me. I was a duckling and followed her where she went, quietly. I was a somber child because pleasing my mother took a lot of energy out of me, and eventually, I learned that her will was stronger than mine, that giving in was a safer, saner route than fighting against her.

She wasn't my birth mother, violent with limbs and words. Ann's tactics were psychological, and they hurt me more than the physical abuses I encountered in all the years before her—with Athanasia and Kristos.

Physical neglect is nothing compared to emotional debasement and depravity, because it's like a poisonous gas you inhale slowly, quietly, not realizing the repercussions until many years later, when you are quietly folding your limbs into the shape of a tennis ball while the man you love screams you into obedience in front of your children. And you quiet down, for them, to end the fight, to end the aching sounds of loathing you hear in his voice, in the words that remind you how insignificant and easily subdued you are.

My mother groomed me for narcissists, transferring my deepest desires to be loved to a man who would love me hard and then squash me even harder, like a bug between his fingertips.

I was obedient. I was a good girl with Ann. When she told me I couldn't speak about my birth family, I enfolded their names, faces, and the memories I held of each of them inside my chest and closed the valves so no one could own the spaces of my heart but Ann.

Stavros, Maria, Nikos, Eleni. My siblings.

John and Athanasia. My parents.

Efthalia. My heart's mother, my aunt.

There was only room for Ann, she told me plainly, and I believed her. I wanted to help her believe me. To help her love me. And if that meant never speaking about them again, it's what I would do. Even though I was eight and couldn't fathom the impact this sacrifice would have on me. Because by erasing them, I was erasing parts of me that Ann did not value, did not want to know. The most honest and pure parts of me. It became a habit when I quashed myself in my marriage for peace, for love.

It makes sense to me, now, why she also changed my name within the first week I lived with her in her home, in her life, as her daughter.

"I want to call you Kathryn," she told me one night as she took a seat on my squeaky mattress. "It was my mother's name, and I want to honor her."

I must have opened my mouth to tell her I was Marina, or perhaps she saw the confusion on my face, because rather quickly, she added, "Your name will still be Marina. It will just be your middle name. Kathryn Marina."

And just like that, in that one moment, I not only lost my family name, Koutrogiannis, but also my birth name. Marina. From that day forward, all my documents claimed me as Kathryn. Marina remained in the middle for a few years, eventually dwindled to an M., and then disappeared completely.

I was just Kathryn, which is defined as purity. I became a blank slate of girlhood, and Ann, because she was my mother, was given the right to rewrite me and re-story me as she desired. To own me in a way that I could not own myself until my fiftieth birthday—when I walked out of my marriage and rewrote myself according to my own needs, my own wants, my own specifications about how people were allowed to live in my life—as guests, not as owners of my body and self.

I don't think Ann really understood what that was like for me, losing my name. It stripped me of my identity, my story, my childhood. Everything that made me Marina was taken from me, including my survival skills—the ones that were sharp and live and booming with electricity—the ones that allowed me to beg on the streets, forage through garbage bins for food, scream at market owners who kicked me out of their stores because I was little and poor, jut my chin at Kristos when he smashed his boombox against my head. I lost the strength my childhood in Greece had fostered out of steel and fire, out of abuse and neglect and abandonment.

I was Kathryn for twenty-five years. Muted. Subdued. A mangled mess of wants and needs Kathryn did not have the language to ask for, to demand.

But this is the girl Ann wanted. The one she sewed together at her vintage Singer machine from the acceptable pieces that belonged to Marina, tossing the spare, unwanted scraps with all their history and pain into the garbage where they belonged. She made Kathryn from scratch, and when I look at this girl in pictures for the next two decades, I only see the muted parts, all the light in her silenced, erased. Only the parts that Ann tolerated from a child were visible. Obedient. Quiet. Submissive. Tolerable.

I didn't become Marina again until I was thirty-three and pregnant with Joseph. Because I wanted my children to know me by my name, I legally took back my name, my identity, through the courts of New York.

"Why don't you just call yourself Marina? Why go through all the trouble of legally changing your name?" These questions came from everyone around me, including a clerk at the law offices I visited, inquiring about the process for taking back my name.

"Because I want my name back. My birth name," my voice cracked. It still cracks when I tell people how I lived by another name, Kathryn, for much of my adolescence and adulthood.

It's also why I use the phrase, "I took back my name" instead of "I changed my name." I didn't change my name. Ann changed my name. I took *back* my name. I reclaimed what was mine, what had been taken from me without permission or consideration. A symbolic rape, a maternal abuse of power.

Ann found out about my name when she came to the hospital to visit her grandson. My documents were all labeled with my name, Marina. Everyone in that setting was calling me Marina. Doped up on pain medication, I said to her, "Oh, I meant to tell you. I'm Marina now. I took my name back."

It wasn't kind. It wasn't nice. But I couldn't talk to her, tell her I had reclaimed my birth name. Undone her steps in reforming and reframing a peasant into a child she could tolerate enough to raise.

My tongue was, and still is, fastened to the vice she fused to my voice when I was eight and nine and twelve and sixteen and twenty-four. I cannot speak to her about my feelings, about growing up with her, about my birth family. An automatic fog replaces logic and voice and sounds and words when she mentions my childhood with her and before her, so that I cannot speak. I lose all access to language. My tongue sits with belligerent stillness at the back of my throat, and I cannot will it forward to help me form words in response to my mother's statements.

All I can muster is, "Uh-huh."

"Oh, you don't want to talk to me about it." She laughs in that way of hers that reminds me I am still willful, still stubborn. That the worst parts of me returned when I assumed my birth name.

But it's not stubbornness that prevents me from talking to her about my childhood, about our relationship. It's a trauma response. I cannot speak. Not to her. My entire body freezes and recoils in her presence, and my voice follows suit when I am on the phone with her. My chest tightens, my bones go cold, and my voice reverts to the safety of silence it has grown accustomed to living in whenever I am near her.

This is the girl she raised. The child she broke. One who cannot speak her truth without her body convulsing with fear, her voice trembling with consternation. Mute. Dumb. Safe.

As harmful as she was in this, however, the emotional state of my growth, when it came down to her sexlessness, Ann was a still safer bet than my birth mother.

Unlike Athanasia's body, which had never belonged to her, Ann's body was never an object of desire, of wanton sex. In possession of an older woman's body that didn't desire companionship, Ann clothed it in drab colors and long, plain lines. She wore simple dresses that she designed on her sewing machine, the hemline of each one resting below her knees, flowing over equally plain black flats. For makeup, she wore only a slight shade of pink lipstick she received for free from the Estee Lauder counter at the mall and a mahogany brown liner for her eyebrows, which she lamented were disappearing. She lived a nun's life, filling the gaps where love and passion would have fit into with travel, museums, Broadway musicals, and friendly luncheons with fellow teachers in Manhattan's best restaurants.

She was sexless, asexual, and for a girl who identified women with the sex that men desired through her birth mother, it was significant when Ann became the mother of my second childhood in the United States. I admired Ann for her control, her detachment from people and love and sex and desire. All of them had been dangerous in my previous life with Athanasia.

I've never told her this. I can't say these things to a woman

I have a challenging time talking to, a woman whose closeness repels me to corners and quick exits.

I spent much of my adolescence like an anthropologist, observing from a distance, taking notes, collecting examples, learning valuable lessons on how to remove myself from a physical space without moving a muscle. How to be there and not be there. How to stitch my emotions into a pocket without seams and how to live among the living, smiling widely and genuinely, without showing that I was drowning in my vomit. How to ask for nothing when I needed so much.

People don't believe me when I tell them Ann is a virgin. She thought kissing was disgusting, and although she named a few dates she went on when younger and a few proposals she declined, she had no interest in men. Getting to know her as an adult, it became clear that no man has known her body or touched her with affection. Her embraces are short-lived, and her kisses touch only the air between her lips and anyone's cheeks.

She has been unloved by men or women, and passion and desire are not words that slip along the sagging lines of her skin, soft and slippery with sex. Hers is not a body willing to unmask itself long enough to be vulnerable. With men or with her daughter.

I know this because after a decade of sex with one man, I too had become sexless, and by the time I turned fifty, no one had touched me with desire for over ten years. Not even my husband. I wouldn't let him.

It is a comfort to own one's body, especially for a woman to own her body in such a way that it does not exist to serve men's needs and wants. My body is my own in the same way my adoptive mother owned and still owns her body, with the same resoluteness with which she owns her house and car and bank accounts. It is less confusing, less of a struggle to possess yourself, to not give pieces of yourself to another human being, to a man who may disappoint you or leave you or live beside you and not see you. A world without men attaching themselves to us — to our bodies — is a world quite free and liberating.

Growing up in this man-less world of Ann's design was a welcome respite from the man-owning existence my first mother introduced to me. In that world, everything belonged to men. Athanasia's small body first belonged to her abusive father, who later returned to reclaim it when she was twenty, and he was released from jail. Then to the men who owned her, occupied her, as if her body were a territory to be claimed and usurped when she was four and eight and sixteen, an indentured servant to the wealthy. Athanasia was kinless, powerless, her voice reduced to a whimper, her will nonexistent.

In marriage, her body belonged to her husband, my father, and then to the five children she birthed and the four children she miscarried, reduced to a machine that took in semen and spit out babies, one after the other, slinking out of her like snakes, because that's what she was supposed to do as a woman. And then it belonged to Kristos, who took ownership not only of my mother, her body, the money she made, and the house my uncle built for her, but also her two daughters and the promise of their bodies when they became of age to sell them.

My mother gave him the rights to all of us when she forfeited the rights to her body and put it in his hands to own and control. He was father, lover, and pimp all in one dark, violent, commanding body of his own.

But in Ann's world, everything belonged to her. Including me. It was a woman's world, and men were not welcome. My body was safe in Ann's world, if not loved or cherished.

A BRIEF HISTORY
OF ANN

*R*ight now, you want to know more about Ann. What happened to her? What experiences made her like this? This is common. Most people who read the articles and books I have dedicated to writing about her want to know more. What traumas did she endure? There must be some explanation for her behavior toward me. Maybe then we can understand her, forgive her even.

I would love to tell you. To lay her down on the table like a cadaver, split her open, and pull apart all the pieces she hid from me. All the bits of her that could explain the enigmatic and precarious woman whose derision has become my internal voice, reminding me again and again of my worthlessness.

But I don't know much about her. The reason my writing about her is nebulous is that I know only the fragments of her I engaged with. Since I write what I know, I can only depict her as I know her. I can write down her words, describe her facial expressions, chronicle the many times she walked away from me, the many weeks and months during which she refused to speak to me, touch me, or even look at me. I didn't exist until the very moment I apologized for whatever infraction I had committed to make her withdraw sight and touch and love from me.

But I don't know much more. My knowledge of her is fractured, limited. Not knowing her, her story, prevents me from understanding her detachment from me. Understanding why she couldn't or wouldn't love me.

This is how she wants it to be between us. She reveals herself only when she wants and only the parts she believes I need to know. But nothing more. She controls her narrative, her history, how much of it I know. She retells the same six to ten stories I have heard in all the years I have known her. There is nothing new. Nothing more, as if that is all there is to her. Ann never told me who she voted for, how much money she deposited in the bank, or what her income was. "That is my private business," she often told me.

She went on vacations without me, like the time she traveled on a cruise to China and didn't share her itinerary with me, when she departed or returned. During that trip, in 1997, there were two earthquakes that hit five major cities in China, and I faced the sting of her friends calling me and asking me about my mother.

"How do you not know how she's doing?" one woman I had never met asked me. "What kind of daughter are you?"

I laughed at that and hung up. I was a distant daughter. That's how Ann wanted it. I didn't know how to find her, how to contact her, and when this was my response to the women she lunched with, they didn't appreciate my lack of information.

But this is the only information I can offer you, also, dear reader. How can I tell you about my second mother when I know even less about her life than that of my birth mother? This is largely why I write myself on paper, in books, in articles. I write my stories and my experiences so my children will know me in ways I have never known—and will never know—my two mothers.

The two most important women in my life are both enigmas to me. Returning to Greece in 1999 helped a little with Athanasia's story. It helped me see her as a victim of sexual abuse, so when she popped five kids out of her body for the sake of her marriage to my father, an older man who only wanted a family—not caring much about who the mother would be or how affected she was because of the abuses she had endured—it helped me see her as someone who could not love me, even if she had wanted to.

Love was not in her arsenal for survival. Only sex was. Male protection was. And the feminine wiles that could afford her both.

I believe that love was a potential tool in Ann's arsenal, but that it was difficult for her to express it. There was and still is a softness to Ann. She smiles. She laughs. She snorts at corny jokes that involve a play on Greek and English words. And she likes to have fun, to travel, to explore gardens and museums and architectural sites in Peru and Bolivia and Ecuador. Her softness has much to do with her insecurity as a woman, a person. Perhaps even as a mother.

Although I was too afraid of her to see her insecurities as a child, I took note of them as an adult. The way she drove in the slowest lane on the highway, twenty miles below the speed limit, cars zipping past her. This was the first time I saw her as an insecure woman and not as a pillar of power and strength. I was twenty-five, had just moved in with Richard, and was teaching high school English.

She didn't scare me anymore. She was a narcissist—having raised me to tend to her feelings, rise to her standards, obey her commands, silence my history—but she wasn't a violent person. A dangerous person. She was just another weak human being usurping power by the spoonful from those she could overpower—children. One child, really.

When it comes to love, she showed it to me the only way she knew how: she adopted me, gave me a roof over my head, bought me used clothes, sent me to school, and fed me. She traveled the globe, got me a passport, and kept me by her side during her expeditions. It's more than I ever received from my birth mother. I was safe with Ann—at least physically. She was a nun, and I was her ward.

How dare I ask for more? She was giving so much more than I ever received before her, so perhaps she was right. I was impossible to please. Desirous of more than the basic needs she fostered between us. Whatever love lived inside her, it was not something that was easily shared, and she chose not to share it with me. After all, I wasn't her natural child. I was an impostor. An outlier. An adopted girl born of roots and genes that did not enthrall or encourage her to love me.

But she did love. That's the thing. She just couldn't love *me*. Not the way I needed to be loved, in that deep way that felt like being safe with someone outside of me. In that deep and loving way I love my own children.

She openly loved her father, George. He was her favorite person, and every time she spoke of him, her face lit up as if she could see him standing beside her, winking at her to ignore her mother, Kathryn, who had a temper. While her mother was a housewife, poor and cranky, her father was jovial and lighthearted, a former wrestler turned barber once he and his family had been kicked out of Turkey for being Greek and found refuge on American soil.

Her parents were kind to a fault, Ann has often told me. "I worked and worked and gave them money, only to find out that they sent my money to their cousins in Greece. Those peasants who didn't deserve it."

Her parents were selfless, poor, and good. And when they died, a year apart from one another, she was left alone, without anyone to care for her, unmoored from the only familial love she knew. It made sense then that she would adopt a child. To give back. To form a family of her own that did not involve sperm or include men, for whom she had no respect. Only two men in her life earned her respect: her father and her cousin Mike.

There is a picture of her with her father that I love to take out of my photo album occasionally and look at. She is standing a few feet away from her dad with a statue rooted to the earth between them. He is a small, overweight man, wearing a coat, smiling at the camera, his double chin resting on the white lapels of his shirt. My mother is about eleven years old and stands opposite him, her eyes drawn to the camera in the same way, but without a smile on her face. Her body is a straight line clothed in shades of black and white and gray, and her eyes are unsmiling. She is frozen to her spot, not angry, not frustrated. Just solemn. Unhappy. Where there is a discernible twinkle in his eyes, playing with the camera, hers are plain, quiet, and vacant.

This is my favorite picture because it reminds me that I am not the one who stole her happiness. Her ability to love and share that love. She was a stark, dark child long before she met me, even while posing for a picture with the only person she has ever admitted to loving. Her father. The only man worthy of her love — this elusive adoration that I have never known from her and have only encountered — in her eyes, in the way they light up and even laugh — when she brings him up.

Her mother has Ann's respect and a different kind of love. A distant kind of love. Maybe the kind of love she has for me. "I won't speak ill of her," she often told me when I asked about her mother — the one whose name she traded mine for. "She was good and kind. She threw a clock at my head once."

"And?" I laughed the first time she told me this because it was such an odd thing to do — and an odd thing to reveal since she often revealed nothing about her childhood to me.

"That's all." I get the sense that her mother was difficult, a cyclone of maternal and feminine tempers, unregulated and aberrant compared to my mother's tepid personality.

Ann is all about control, never showing herself. Just as I never felt safe enough with her to tell her about my childhood evils, she never felt safe enough with me to tell me about hers. We lived together for seventeen years, knowing only the surface of each other's pain. Never the interior. Never the deep, muddy parts I hunt down and pick at with my fingertips in the people I love, like Richard—when we first met—like my kids, my friends.

It's that hidden stuff I want to touch and know. The elusive, painful parts that meet mine halfway, and instead of rejection, we find mutual love, empathy, a need to protect and safeguard the hurts everyone else has left behind.

"Ask her," you nudge me. I can feel your fingertips digging into my arm, pushing me toward my mother, as if asking her will open the doors to forgiveness and acceptance that up to this point in our relationship have been fruitless.

And all I can say to you is, I can't.

She is ninety-two and still guarded with her heart. Dementia fog has burrowed into her memories like a tick rummaging through matted hair for a blood source. The only images she projects to me are those she has always projected to me. The same ones. None are different or new.

She had a lamb. Her uncle threatened to kill and prepare it for dinner, and she ran away for about a minute before they found her and brought her back to the house. They served the lamb for dinner, but she refused to eat it.

She was adopted, too. She found out as an adult. Her mother's sister Maria, the same one I lived with during my adoption, told her she was the daughter of a cousin who was too poor to raise any more children, so Kathryn, who couldn't have kids of her own, took her. Her parents never told her the truth.

Before going into teaching, perhaps for the stability of income and retirement money, she was all about fashion. Ann designed shop windows during the Christmas season for top-of-the-line stores lined up along Manhattan's streets. She also worked as a set designer for two male photographers who paid her well. Although she wasn't as pretty as the models in the shoots, the men used her hands, fragile, feminine, and elegant, for some pictures. There is a black-and-white photograph of Ann straightening out the billowy skirts of a model right before the photo shoot. She was smiling, having fun.

She was in love with one of the photographers. But he wasn't interested in her. He dated one of the models instead. Ann quit. Left the business for good, and the romantic writer in me has determined that this was when her heart broke, because of this man. Unable to repair it herself, she ran away, fractured and rejected, refusing to trust again, to fall in love again.

That's the story I tell of her, but it's my narrative. Not hers. She doesn't share the interior layers of her failures, her heartbreaks. Not with me. I'm not sure with anyone. Her heart has been Bubble Wrapped and then cemented for good measure. No one can crack her open and sift through the layers to get to the warm and mushy center of her heart. She won't let you. She never let me.

After a career in photography, she took her money, bought a summer house for her parents in Stonybrook, and began teaching elementary school. Ann returned to school, received her master's in science education and began teaching middle school science. Then high school science. At sixty-five, she graduated with a master's in library science, worked in a school library for two years, and then retired for good.

My mother is artistic, too. In her retirement, she threw herself into cooking and baking, piano lessons, quilting, and arts and crafts. I have a collection of bookmarks, greeting cards, and Christmas tree ornaments she crafted—intricate, lovely pieces of art—and passed on to me and the kids.

She was a pioneer, a feminist without subscribing to the

feminist tenets of the time. She lived in France for a year, worked for Anne Klein, and spoke French fluently. She proudly told me she had been one of the first women to wear jeans when women were still expected to wear dresses and skirts. She was the only woman enrolled in nautical law courses and combated sexism from her professors and male peers, which only goaded her to remain in the program when any other woman would have dropped out. When she did drop out, it was to adopt me in 1979, which made her one of the first women of her time to attempt adoption without a husband or other man by her side. In the seventies, a single woman adopting a child on her own, being able to afford to do so, was an unheard-of scenario.

Today, after two consecutive heart attacks in one month, a three-week stay in the hospital, followed by a three-year COVID pandemic, she is still thriving. She is weaker, on daily doses of heart medication, and without a cardiologist to care for her because she keeps firing them one after the other for a variety of reasons that made them untenable for her. They charge too much. They don't call her back when she calls them. They make her take too many unnecessary tests to rack up insurance money, which makes them corrupt and immoral. They expect her to visit them once a month, which is too much. In one year, she hired and fired six cardiologists between Queens and Manhattan. She no longer takes the train to the city, relying on the bus or senior citizen organizations and vans to take her shopping, or to her regular physician's office, the only one she trusts to call in her drug prescriptions.

Ann knows she's going to die. It's only a matter of when. In terms of kin, she's down to me and Richard. Richard, really, because when I asked her to stop speaking with him during my divorce and revealing my financial situation to him, she told me in that frank and callous way of hers, "You can't tell me who I can be friends with or who I can call."

"But I'm your daughter," I explained to her. "You should be loyal to me, not your ex-son-in-law. We have a contentious relationship, and it doesn't help that you tell him about my financial hardships. He uses them against me."

"Well, that is between you and him. That is none of my business. I have a separate relationship with him."

How do I explain to her that her love for me should supersede her need for him, a man she loathed and refused to call by his name until after we were married and had kids? How do you explain to someone, your family, that you should be loved first, not the ex-husband you walked away from because of his rage and derision for you?

How do you explain love and loyalty to someone—your own mother—who never possessed those feelings for you?

I couldn't. I can't, even now.

Because Ann never loved me. Not the way I deserve to be loved. And my life's journey, to this day, points to this missing piece in my life: love. Not romantic love. Not marital love. But the love a parent has for her child. I possess love for my children, but the days of mothering me have come and gone, and I have been unloved by my mothers. Since I now understand that I will never earn her love, the one from whom I have been seeking love since the age of eight, there is only one mother left to love me.

Me. Any love that I need now must come from me.

This is all I know.

And this is all I know of Ann, too, and all I will ever know about her. It's not satisfying, for you or for me. But imagine being me, her daughter of forty-two years, still unable to put a dent in the hard, steely shell she wore over the fragile persona I grew up hoping to grab hold of and love with the intensity that breathes inside me.

She will die one day soon, not knowing who I am. Without

seeing me as worthy of her affections. Not knowing that the girl and woman she has rejected ad nauseam still only wants one thing from her: to be loved.

Maybe even to be seen.

TOUCH-STARVED

*A*nn starved me in ways I did not know one person could starve another. There was food in the refrigerator, clothes on my back, a school to attend, and a roof over my head. These were basic and consistent and everything I did not have when I was Athanasia's daughter.

But there were no outward displays of affection, and this starvation was more harrowing than digging through garbage cans for food, which I did as the daughter of my first mother.

"I love you," I told her as young as eight, not because I loved her—I'd just met her—but because I wanted to hear the words back, to feel that in adopting me, she loved me. Had chosen me.

"Thank you," she responded, her mouth in a tight smile.

I waited for the next words I knew should come, but I waited in vain. They never came.

We played this game until I was thirteen, and then it stopped, fading away like worn jeans that don't quite fit the curves every adolescent girl develops. I outgrew the lie. And I already knew the answer. She didn't love me back.

The first and only time she told me she loved me, I was thirty-three and had just given birth to my son, Joseph. We were on the phone, and she repeated the phrase she now recites as often and with the same urgency as I used to tell her I loved her: "I know you think I was a terrible mother." Not "I was a terrible mother," but "I know you think." It's all on me.

"You did your best," I told her. I still tell her, understanding that at ninety-two and living by herself in New York, she wants to set the record straight. A mother of nineteen years myself, I realize how hard it is to be a mother, to parent kids whose needs do not present themselves in words written across their foreheads.

She did her best. I do my best. I have forgiven her for her emotional denial and starvation and no longer have any need to hear those words. Not from her.

I hear them every day from my children, but unlike Ann, I don't let them tell me first. I tell them first, five times a day. And when they are too angry to hear the words, their hands crossed against their chests, willing my words to hit the walls they want to put between us, I show them the depths of my love. I force-feed them love. I grab them, pull them to me, and hug away the darkness I planted in their bosoms. I turn my gaze to them, love them with my eyes, let them see the devotion living there without conditions, reservations, or expectations.

I am a different mother, despite my own failings — and we all fail when we endeavor to meet the needs of others. We can't possibly meet everyone's needs all the time. Some needs go unmet until they find someone else to meet them. A teacher. A lover. A friend. A boyfriend. We all make do. We all find what we need. In the end.

"I know you think I don't love you, but I do," she repeated over the phone line. Hugging my son to my chest, I said, "I know," even though I really didn't.

I didn't stop there. "It didn't always feel like you did. You withheld your love from me when we were on the trip in the Poconos, when I told the little boy I was adopted."

"Yes," she said without a pause while my son nestled into the curve of my breasts in ways I was never allowed to enjoy comfort in the bodies of my two mothers. "I did withhold love from you."

The admission ripped open my old wounds, and I sat there

on my couch, miles away from her, rocking my son, mute from the aftershock of her confession. There was no apology. No shame in the admission.

She was so angry with me on that trip that she ushered me into her car and drove us back to Queens from Pennsylvania in the middle of the night. I remember her ordering me to stay in the car, as if she were ashamed of me, while she walked to the main office to return our cabin keys to the park workers. I curled my ten-year-old body into the reclined seat in the car, hiding from anyone who might see us leave, as if I had committed a crime.

But there had been no crime. A little boy I befriended asked me where my father was, and after a series of responses that didn't satisfy his curiosity, I confessed: "I'm adopted. I have a father, but he left us; my family put me up for adoption, and here I am, with a new mother." He was quiet after that, and we continued to twirl our small bodies over the railing until we were upside down and laughing at each other's awkwardness.

Several hours later, seated in the dining hall, I watched my mother go to the buffet table for more salad. The little boy's mother stopped her, whispered something in her ear, and patted her arm. I knew I was in trouble. I had said too much. Revealed too much about myself. About her. My mother returned to the table, took my plate, and told me we were leaving.

I had committed an unspeakable crime. By speaking. By telling my truth: that she was not my birth mother.

Adopting a child is never a crime. I was always proud to tell people I was adopted. I was proud of her, too, for adopting me, for giving me a second chance at life by snatching me out of homelessness and depravity to show me I could build a new life for myself, detached from the debris of my upbringing.

But for Ann, my adoption was a secret she wanted to hide in the vault at the bank, along with the cross my father gave me before I left him. A cross with the protruding figure of Jesus pinned to it, my full Greek name inscribed in gold on the back: Marina Koutrogiannis. It was the only object that accompanied me to the United States, an artifact of everything I left behind.

I cried the first night I spent in her home, lying on the new bed that was mine, in the room that would belong to me until my twenty-fifth birthday, until I found the courage to leave her.

"I miss my baba," I told her in Greek, between the stream of sobs and hiccups rushing out of me. I felt her body withdraw from mine, and with more than a few inches between us, my new mother told me something I did not know. Something I did not want to believe.

"Your father is the one who gave you away, you know." Her eyes, cold and distant, were struck by the streetlight sneaking between the curtains in my room, as if showing me her true nature was important. I held my breath, wanting to hear her next words as much as I needed to see who she was, how far she would go.

"He was there, at the courthouse, when I adopted you. He signed the papers to give you up." She patted my knee and rose from my bedside, the movement leaving behind a fissure of cold air, my skin prickling with anticipation.

After she left my room and closed the door behind her, I slipped under my covers, hiding in the dark, my body retiring into itself, and realized she had taken my father away from me. She might as well have told me, "He didn't want you." It was all the same to me.

I loved my baba until that moment—his tenderness, the last days I spent with him, walking about his neighborhood, eating souvlaki, and listening to the soft and quiet movements of his body alongside my own. But now I knew he was the one who had given me away. It all made sense—the visits, the walks, the adoption.

I stopped loving him that day. All of me began to forget him in slow but sure degrees, like a flame dying out on its own, the wick burned beyond recognition, so it could never be relit. I stopped crying and lay there, still and numb, digesting the messages my body sent me, the warning signs triggered by my new mother's words.

"You can't trust her," it whispered so my mother wouldn't hear. "Be careful with her."

I half-listened. My desire to be loved by her was a siren call hurling me against the currents and smashing me into the sharp stones of disappointment, again and again, amnesia taking over every time I threw myself at my mother and she threw me back against the jagged edges of denial.

My new mother wanted no one outside her family to know I was adopted. I pretended she was my birth mother, even though she looked like my grandmother with her white hair and rolling hips. She wanted me to pretend I had no father, no other mother. That I was a single child. A fatherless child. A bastard was better than an adopted child. I couldn't even name my siblings. The childhood I lived before her—with all the harrowing experiences strapped to my chest like a bomb vest sewn into the lining of my skin—was unutterable. To breathe any of it into the air risked losing her affections.

Ann starved my body, too. She never held or caressed it. Her body was not a body in which I found solace or comfort. There was a wall as thick and formidable as marble standing between us.

I grew up often watching Ann's hands, loving them, partly because of how out of reach they were to me. Her fingers, long and feminine in contrast to my short, stubby ones, were gentle and guileless, and I was transfixed by their grace, the way the pinky plucked the air when she drank coffee or tea, the way beautiful and rare stones affixed on gold and silver bands brought out the tan highlights of her skin, freckles sprouting like little stars ascending toward her wrist and disappearing beneath the folds of her sleeves.

My eyes often fell to her hands when she reproached me as a child, reminding me of how I fell short, how I resembled not her but my birth mother, the whore who had given birth to me and passed me on to Ann. I sat before her mute, my eyes glistening with tears, searching for something more of her in her hands, hands I wished would glide over my hair, touch my face, love me in the physical ways she couldn't love anyone.

While her words were harsh and her eyes distant, her hands told another story about Ann. If they were gentle, lovely, there had to be another part of her as gentle, as lovely, and I drowned myself in those hands without touching her, willing them to reveal a side she hid behind endless rigidity, emotional estrangement, and self-containment.

Three Decembers ago, after her second heart attack, I found myself watching those same hands, still long and gentle in appearance, wrinkled by time, trembling with age as she reached out to pick up her coffee cup. I stared at those hands, hands I've grown to adore while resenting the woman attached to them, wishing they would adore me back, caress me in places only a mother would know to touch. Places my own fingers touch my daughter. Her hair, the small of her back, down her arms, the length of her fingertips, the inside of her palms.

Because my mother never touched me, I know where to touch my daughter, how to soothe her when she is without words, her emotions running out of her mouth in garbled sobs. I have learned how to touch, soothe, love because of the absence of all these sustaining and nurturing qualities denied me.

I often chased my son, when he lived at home, following his sounds when he sauntered from room to room like a ghost, only coming out of his bedroom for a snack or to run his fingers along the black-and-white keys of our piano, his eyes closed, his long, thin frame swaying to the rhythms of nurturance he found in music. I used to sit on the staircase, hidden by the half wall that stood between us, listening, watching, feeding myself with the sight of him, loving him with my eyes.

Preparing himself for the journey of moving out and going off to college, he learned to detach himself from us, fending for himself. But I didn't want him to go off feeling untouched, unloved, so I waited until he was in the kitchen getting a snack, or after he finished his Chopin, and then I moved into him, wrapped my arms around his bony frame, and reached up to plant a noisy kiss on his cheek.

Gentle and sweet, Joseph's hands reciprocate, even today, wrapping around me for a hug. His lips always touch my own cheek, and this is when I know he is not touch resistant—as much as he wants his space and privacy to grow into himself, he needs human touch and love. Still. Always, I hope.

Ann never enfolded me into her body the way I take my daughter's body into mine, my son's, cocooning them in the safety I hope they will always find in my mothering of them. Touch is a way to nourish the ones we love. It's food, fuel. To not know touch—the good, safe kind of touch our parents ought to give us— is negligence, starvation.

My body and I have not known touch like that, not from our mothers. To think about my childhood, all of it, before Ann and during Ann's reign, is to know the absence of touch.

WHEN HUNGRY GIRLS
MEET HUNGRY MEN

*G*rowing up in a house without being caressed, being raised by a woman who did not reach out to hug me or kiss me or touch my arm, my hair, left gaping holes in me, in my body. Holes I still don't know how to fill outside of the love and care I show my kids.

I give them what I didn't get and was not given, cognizant also of the holes yawning and stretching along their limbs without the words to articulate with what kind of nurturance they need those holes to be fed. I guess, desperately filling their empty baskets as I used to fill their Easter and Halloween baskets, with goodies and hugs and kisses, with *how are you*s? and *I love you*s, and *what can I do for you*? and *how are you feeling today*? Overfeeding them in the hopes that some of what I give them is what they need in that moment. Hoping if I feed them enough and anticipate their needs, their holes won't be filled by someone else, someone inappropriate, someone looking for those holes and pains to usurp and take advantage of them the way Mr. Schwartz anticipated mine.

My adoptive mother's hands, absent from me, were replaced by the much older, trembling hands of my violin teacher. He was seventy to my eleven, and even now, I wonder how perpetrators know how to find little girls and boys to mishandle. How do they find us—those of us so hungry for touch and love that we end up sitting right in front of them, full of yearnings we haven't learned to give voice to yet?

Mr. Schwartz was my teacher for a year, watching me, I suppose, quietly assessing whether I was the kind of child who would tell or scream or make a fuss. I wasn't. I was the quiet one. I listened to him, placed my fingers where he bade me on the violin strings, held the bow as he showed me, with rigid obedience. I only spoke when spoken to, smiled when coaxed, and kept my eyes focused on my violin when I slid the bow across the strings, on his thick fingers when they modeled a scale on his violin, and on his shoes when he addressed me.

Men disappeared from my life when I was taken away from my birth mother's chaotic spaces, full of the lechery and sex Kristos brought to our doorstop. I was safe with Ann, because men did not revolve around her life, and therefore, did not sneak into mine. I suppose in the sights of the Greek gods doling out suffering and respite for us lowly folk, they thought reprieve from sexual volatility was enough. After all, we can't have it all. Safety *and* love. Safety was good enough for me, albeit lonely and isolating without love.

So how was it that Mr. Schwartz, a Jewish refugee from Austria, was able to see that love was missing in me? That I was a good target for his undoing the knots of my reconstructed innocence?

For the first few months during my lessons, my mother sat outside my lesson studio, on one of the hallway benches reserved for parents. But eventually, once she felt I was safe with him, she stopped coming into the building with me. She dropped me off, went food shopping, and waited for me outside the building, her green Chevy double-parked along the congested Woodhaven Boulevard.

He waited until he was sure this would be a pattern—her not

sitting outside the room, her ears pricking at the sound of my bow squealing against the strings to mimic music — before he revealed himself to me.

"Why do you look so sad?" he asked me, taking a seat opposite me, his thick legs creaking as they bent beneath him.

"I had a fight with my mom," I told him. He smiled. He always started our lessons with small chats, to get to know me, to ease me into playing duets.

"What about?" His eyes were concentrating on my violin, his fingers plucking at the strings as he tuned it.

I shrugged my shoulders.

"You can tell me." He looked at me, reassuring me with a slow smile that showed me his yellowed teeth, straight but decaying. "What you say here, stays here."

My heartbeat bounced like a firecracker, ricocheting against my rib cage. I didn't like talking about my mother. If she found out, she would hate me again. But he was kind and looked at me with the same level of patience he often showed me while my fingers struggled to find the correct section of the violin strings when I played for him.

"Well, I want a better allowance, but she won't give me anything more than twenty-five cents a week. She thinks I'm going to buy drugs with it."

He said nothing. Instead, he extended his right leg forward, placed his thick fingers into his pocket, and took out a wad of bills. He pulled a twenty-dollar bill from it and handed it to me.

"Here you go," he said. "Take it. Buy yourself something nice."

I looked at the bill. It was the same one I'd given him when I first came into his office. I'd watched him take it from my hand and place it over the other bills he stuffed into his pocket.

"I can't take your money. That's for my lesson."

He pried my fingers from my sides, opened my palm, and

placed the bill into them. "It's my gift to you. Whenever you need money, you come to me. I will give it to you."

I said nothing, wishing I had kept my mouth shut. Then I wouldn't be here, in this situation. I wanted to give the money back to him, turn back the time, and return to my actual lesson. To the way it was before, all ritualized and impersonal. Now it was personal. Money made it personal. Awkward. Dare I say, *intimate*.

I watched him, the bill still held inside my fist, it seems, from a distance. He put my violin and bow on top of the piano, pulled the legs of his pants up as he sat deeper into his chair, and tapped his fingers on his knees. "Come. Sit. Let's talk."

My pulse quickened and a heavy vibration filled my ears, the way it sounds when you place a conch shell to them and listen for the deep sounds of the ocean. I didn't hear his voice when he repeated his bidding again. I only saw his lips moving, felt his large fingers pull me to him, lift me onto his lap, shift his legs open to welcome me into his hips.

My body froze then, like a doll hoisted upon a shelf, stiff and stoic, upright and rigid, lest it fall from its great height. Not a muscle shifted as his fingers inched their way down the small length of my back, pried the hem of the T-shirt off my skin, and buried themselves beneath it. My skin was soft then, unmarred by the acne that would plague my teen years, make me feel like a leper, punished for some great indignity of my own making. Like this one. For not being careful. For not fighting back the way I used to fight against Kristos.

I wasn't new to this. I knew about men—the menacing ones. I knew to stay away from them. I sensed them the way dogs sense danger through their noses and the pores breathing beneath the matted hairs of their fur. But I hadn't anticipated this. Hadn't expected it to happen to me here, in New York, so far away from the life I had known in Athens so many years earlier. Was I safe anywhere? With anyone? Could no one be trusted? Not even my seventy-year-old Austrian violin teacher?

I held my breath while his hands took their time to know the skin holding me together, my insides in chaos, as if being let loose during a house fire, running blindly, searching for clean air to inhale amid burning debris and stifling smoke. I did not move. I did not say a word. My eyes were glued to the door, half-willing my mother to storm in and save me, wondering where she was and why she trusted this man enough to leave me alone with him, with the door closed, the sounds of violin music muted by its thickness.

When he was done, I hugged the silence between us and stood still as he removed his hand from beneath my shirt, patted my knee, and shifted in his seat, letting me know I could climb off his thighs.

He was done with me. It was time for his next lesson.

When I didn't move to place my violin and bow in the case, he did this for me, my eyes feeling his movements but not directly seeing them. He opened the door, and I walked out into the hallway, not inhaling a breath again until I was outside and saw my mother's car waiting for me with her in it.

The following week, my lesson was the same. Except there was no preamble, no introduction. No pretenses a violin would be played, or a music lesson would be learned—or taught. I walked in, he put my violin on the floor beside him, sat down on the chair, and motioned for me to take my place on his lap.

There were no words between us, and the noises in the room consisted of his hands rubbing against the skin of my bare back. There was no bra to unhook or fidget with. I was only eleven and still flat, but in those thirty minutes, my lesson learned was that no man could be trusted—not even the old, seemingly kind ones.

His lesson was the study of my back, where the bones protruded, how my skin softened along the length of my spine, how his touch birthed goosebumps to rise and meet his fingertips at the nape of my neck. It was a betrayal, the chill that overtook my body, and I hated it for responding to his touch.

I broke away from him without moving, without shifting. I wasn't there, on his lap, surrendering to his hands. I was a vacant lot made of nothing more than skin and bones. My body did not belong to me. I abandoned it.

When he let me go this time, he handed me another twenty-dollar bill. It struck me then that he saw me—a little girl—just as men had seen my birth mother.

I realized how easy it is to make whores of girls and how easy it is to become one. A whore. A prostitute. That men felt entitled to our bodies and paid us for the touch of them. The feel of them. It doesn't matter if we are eleven or twenty or forty-five. Girls only have one purpose. To please men. With or without our consent.

And didn't I consent? He paid for me. I took the money.

It doesn't matter that I tore both bills to shreds and chucked them into the garbage bin as soon as I got home. I still took them. I sat on his lap, not once, but twice.

It doesn't matter that I didn't move, that I didn't like it, that I sat as still as a dead fly. I still sat on his lap. I didn't scream or punch him or spit in his face or run out of his office. I stayed. I even went back.

Why?

What is this power he had over me—this power that bid me not to tell, not to scream, not to resist? To sit there while his hands consumed me, memorized me, reminded me of my place in this world. A whore. A sex thing. Like my birth mother.

How much did men pay to touch her? How old was she the first time she learned her body could earn money?

I didn't go back to Mr. Schwartz the following week. And I didn't tell my mother what he did. What I did. I still haven't. I concocted a plan instead to save me, to keep me out of his hands before they crawled toward my chest, which I am sure was his ultimate destination, if not farther.

I told my mother I needed a new teacher, that as good as he was, I wasn't learning theory. I needed theory to be a concert violinist, I reminded her, since this was her dream for me even though I only practiced for fifteen minutes a day to a baking timer set by her own hands. By my next lesson, I was enrolled in a music program at Queens College, where my private lessons occurred with a young graduate student—a female, this time. I began to insist on women for anything that required me to be behind closed doors with other humans—doctors, teachers, nurses.

Ann did not deny me this, but she also never asked why. I'm not sure I would have told her. She didn't believe me when I told her about my mother, her pimp, the abuse, the hunger. These were tall tales to her, earning me the indignity of being called a liar.

I didn't think she would believe that my violin teacher, as old as he was, had taken her money to grope me. I knew she would believe that I'd asked for it in some way, like telling him she wouldn't give me an allowance. Or taking the money. Sitting on his lap. Not fighting back.

I told her nothing. I kept it to myself and found another way to protect my body from further corruption.

When I was in college, I was on the subway train headed to work and bumped into the daughter of the couple that managed Mr. Schwartz and the school for which he worked.

"I have some bad news," she told me, her manicured fingers clutching my arm as the train jostled us back and forth, like loose ice cubes in a cocktail glass. "Mr. Schwartz passed away a few months ago. He was your teacher, right? What a loss. He was such a nice man."

I pulled at the muscles on my face as if pulling taffy apart, forcing a stiff smile and a nod.

He groped me during my lessons, I wanted to tell her. But the words would not come out.

What did it matter? He was dead. Good riddance. What does it matter now to tell her he groped me years ago when I was little? It wouldn't change a thing. He died with a stellar reputation and took his depravity with him to his grave.

I wondered how many other children he groped in his music room with the door closed, his Austrian accent buffering the greed and lust into the dulcet tones of kindness and compassion he used to betray us. How many of us walk around like ghosts carrying the dead weight of our innocence strapped to our backs, corrupted by the adults we were told to trust?

But what does it matter? These men die noble deaths while we live on, trying to scratch off the trauma they inscribed onto our bodies, the memory of their fingers tattooed to our skin, permanently scarred, burning with self-loathing.

We belong to them, too, just as our bodies did. After all, they paid for us, in one way or another. They pay and they take. And we're left behind to remember how defenseless we were.

How feminine.

How sexed.

PRETTY LITTLE
WAIF GIRL

"You look like a waif," Ann told me when I was in middle school. And high school and college, for that matter. "You look old and used up. You should take better care of yourself."

These were the phrases I grew up with in my home with Ann. She never told me I was beautiful or pretty. She only rolled her brown, knowing eyes over the small curves of my body and reminded me of my failings. My origins.

"If you keep this up," she told me as young as eleven, simply for going roller-skating with my friends, or being an hour late coming home from school, or being grumpy in her presence, "you'll end up just like your mother. A *putana*." A whore.

"You're my mother," I shot at her, hoping she got the gist of my implication. *Are you calling yourself a whore?* was not a phrase that slipped out of my mouth, but it was in the breath of poisoned space lingering between us that neither one of us dared address or inhale.

"We both know that's not true," she shot back and walked away, happy to remind me I did not come from her, did not belong to her. Telling me she was not my mother hurt much more than calling me a whore. It cut deeper, this denial, leaving behind a hollowness in me I have yet to fill to my satisfaction.

I never looked up the word *putana*. I knew what it meant

because my birth mother was one, and I grew up hearing men and women calling her that as if it were her nickname. I also knew my adoptive mother wanted to remind me of my birth mother's profession in case I ended up like her. If I ended up being a whore, it wouldn't be Ann's fault. It was in my genes.

But waif was a different term, and she used this term to define me well into my twenties.

Waif comes from the Old French *guaif*, translated as "stray beast." Is this how she saw me? A stray? A beast? A wild animal she couldn't tame?

Waif is also defined as "a homeless, neglected, or abandoned person, especially a child."

Another dictionary writes that a waif is a young person who is thin and looks unhealthy and uncared for.

So the signs were there. Ann saw them. She even named them. I was homeless, abandoned, uncared for. And even though she adopted me and gave me a home, I continued to look uncared for and unhealthy in her care.

In calling me a waif, she put the blame on me. It was my fault I looked this way. It was my doing.

But I was eight. And eleven. And fifteen. I had no agency then. I only had a mother who saw the signs and didn't do anything about them. Perhaps she didn't know what they meant. That I came from a place of corruption and abuse and was not being given the tools with which to understand them and how they belonged to me. But then again, when I was thirteen and graduated from middle school, the idea of seeing a therapist did come up.

I cut school on my last day as an eighth grader. My best friend and I decided to skip lunch and recess. We went to Farida's home, where we listened to music and she put makeup on my face, brushed my hair, and sprayed it in place. When I looked in the mirror, I didn't recognize myself. My eyes were dark and popped out of my face, not like a waif's, but like one of the beautiful images of girls we found in teen magazines. There was a spot of pink blush on both cheeks and red lipstick made the twin lines on my face seem loud, vibrant, and kissable. I looked pretty, like a girl a boy would want to look at and even think about kissing. A pretty waif.

By the time we returned to school, we had missed our homeroom class, which meant I would be going home without my report card. When my mom learned this, she left me at home, drove to my school, picked up my report card, saw that I received an *F* in English, no less, and refused to attend my graduation. I went without her, and to get back at her, I refused to stand when everyone was instructed to stand for the parents who supported our progress in school, seeing us through to our graduation day.

What made this laughable was that I was in the band, seated front and center on the stage, my clarinet between my knees. I was the only one who remained seated in a whole auditorium of upright moms, dads, teachers, and students. If my mother had been there, she wouldn't have missed me. But she wasn't. She kept her promise not to show up for me because I disobeyed her by being friends with Farida, whom she did not like, for cutting school, for coming home with a made-up face, and for failing English, the only subject I was good at.

"I want to see a therapist," I told her afterward, knowing that I needed to talk to someone, anyone that was not her.

"I'll take you to one," she told me, looking out the window, over her shoulder.

"I want you to go with me," I pleaded, not going into details. I was desperate. I needed to understand why she treated me the way she did. What I did to make me so unlovable. Why thoughts of dragging knives along my veins became everyday occurrences that kept me awake at night and daydreaming during the day.

She shook her head. "No. I will take you, but I will not go to one." Pause. "I hope you're not going to talk about me."

"About you and about me. But we should talk to someone. Together." I softened my voice, seeing a light in this otherwise dark tunnel that had grown between my new mother and me. I needed a professional to fix us. Neither one of us had the tools to repair the damage that fed on our relationship.

She looked at me then, cocking her head to the right, her eyes pointed at me like darts, her eyebrows high, her lips shaped into a grim gloat that told me I was a lost cause and we both knew it. Or that this was all my fault, and we both knew it.

"I don't need a therapist. People know what's wrong with them." She walked away from me then and scurried back into her bedroom, closed the door, and let me know not to interrupt her by the clicking sound of the lock that spoke to me for her.

The subject never came up again, and she never took me to a therapist. Ensuring I did not have the opportunity to talk about her with a stranger was more important than my emotional health.

Ann may have known what was wrong with her, but I was around the corner of thirteen then. I had my feelings and her rejections to contend with, and I didn't understand any of them.

When my mother looked at me, she didn't see the pain and the longing. She only saw the waif in me, without making the necessary connection that pain was the logical corollary of my waif-hood.

I didn't wear makeup. I wore baggy clothes, baggy shirts. Nothing tight or revealing ever touched my skin. Even my skin was hidden. My chocolate-brown hair hung limply down to my shoulders, resting there like untouched strings. I had bangs, sometimes long enough to cover my eyes, which made me look more waif-like than usual.

I still have my bangs, at fifty, unable to imagine myself without them. Like my glasses, they serve as a protective shield, a veil of brown that stands between me and onlookers. My waist is thicker, my belly rounded, and my face has aged, but I still feel like a twelve-year-old. I am stuck there, as if that is when I stopped developing. The year I killed myself, my psyche, even though I was not able to rid myself of my physical body.

I tried not to look into mirrors in those days. There was one oval mirror attached to my dresser, and I came face-to-face with it when I collected my clothing each morning, but our eyes never met. I would investigate the glass and look over my shoulder, or at the stain on my jeans, but I avoided my own gaze. What would I see there? I already knew how I felt in my skin, carrying my body around like a heavy weight I couldn't surrender.

When I was eighteen and worked at the local library as a page, a job I acquired at the age of sixteen, assigned to put books away according to the Dewey decimal system, the head supervisor asked me into her office. I thought I was in trouble because I'd been in the habit of arriving at work late. I often snuck into my post through the back door, in the hopes that the librarians wouldn't see me enter, and tucking myself behind a bookshelf, pretending I had been there the whole time.

"You should do something nice to your hair. Put some makeup on," Mrs. Zimmerman added. She was older, in her mid-sixties, and the head librarian. She was tiny, shorter than my five-foot-one frame, but her dyed blond hair was always up in an elegant bun, and her thick form was adorned with necklaces and dresses vibrant with pink and orange hues. She was feminine with short heels to complete the ensemble of her femaleness.

"You're very attractive, but you should put some care into yourself. It will make you feel better."

I remember my body growing cold in her office, rigid with tension. This woman had never said two words to me other than "good night" or "good morning," and here she was assuming intimacy with me.

Plus. I didn't care how I looked. I looked the way I felt. Wasted. Discarded. Unloved. Putting on a pretty face would not give me what I hungered for most. A mother. Those feelings of love that I glimpsed on television shows and sometimes between parents and their children at the library or among my friends but never encountered myself.

"Is that all?" I asked her, looking over her rounded shoulders and out of the window frame behind her. I gazed at the row of trees that protruded from the gray concrete of the street outside, my breathing syncing with the swaying branches that lulled my insides into a state of numbness.

"Yes," she said, smarting at my coldness and correcting her posture as she straightened her back against her leather chair.

"Thanks," I told her as I rose from the seat opposite her wide executive desk and left the office. I went back into the stacks, hiding there for the rest of my shift, running my fingertips over the titles and names of authors I had yet to meet, making a list of the books I intended to read over the summer before putting them back into their homes as if they had not been disturbed by my curiosity.

She didn't know me. If she had, she'd have known that I didn't like dressing up like a girl. Pretty girls drew attention, male attention, and I didn't like that kind of attention. That included wearing skirts, which I loathed. Every Easter, my mother made me a dress on her Singer sewing machine, forced me to try it on while she placed pins at the hem of its skirt, and asked me to stop fidgeting for the umpteenth time.

"I don't like wearing dresses," I told her again. Dresses made me feel girly, and there was nothing girly about me. I didn't paint my nails or brush my hair—except once after taking a shower. I didn't like wearing nice shoes or pantyhose, and I certainly didn't like those ridiculous Greek Easter bonnets she bought me every April.

"You need to look like a lady," Ann instructed me through the string of pins she clenched between her lips.

"I'm not a lady. I'm a kid. And I hate dresses." I clasped my arms around my middle, as if my stomach hurt, but quickly returned them to the side like two stiff sticks when she arched her eyebrows at me with disapproval.

I spent much of my childhood stuffed into dresses against my will. Not at school. At school, I was allowed to dress myself, dragging my body from class to class, masked in jeans and sneakers and bulky sweaters that I could disappear into, my fingers buried into the sleeves, coming out only to find refuge in my mouth when I needed to chew the nails and the skin around the red, throbbing mounds of my fingers. But at church on Sundays, I had to wear a dress. And on graduation days from elementary school, middle school, high school, and on Easter. On public days, when I could not be seen as a waif by those who knew my mother, I had to dress like a lady. A pretty girl that had nothing to do with me and how I felt inside.

I don't know where my aversion to feminine dressing came from, but it was there long before I took notice of it. I hadn't worn a dress in my childhood before Ann, and I was quite set against it during her reign. Perhaps it's because the feminine was a scary place for me, a place threaded with intimacy, men, and sex.

Perhaps they reminded me of my birth mother, hiking up her skirts while sitting on public benches, drawing johns' eyes to the deep contours of her thighs. Or the red stilettos she slipped her feet into when she went out on "dates" with the motorcycle man while still married to our father—the ones that crowd my first memory of their fight, the red heel glistening with my father's blood after it struck his eye.

To this day, I cannot wear red. It reminds me of sex. Of her red stilettos. Of my father's blood rolling down his face after she struck him.

Dressing up in skirts and makeup and heels seemed like a thing women did to make themselves attractive to men, and I didn't want any of that. Not as a girl and not as a young adult.

I was nineteen going on twenty when wearing dresses and makeup and heels overcame me for a while. I was friends with Jannipp, a Puerto Rican girl I met while working at a jeans store in the mall. She was very girly, her dark features lit up with bright hues of red and pink and blue makeup, tight jeans and miniskirts hugging her stick-thin hips, complete with high heels that matched her outfits. Her clothing screamed sex appeal, the loud and vibrant colors of her outfits and personality never quite mixing with the brown-and-black hues of my own attire. My dark colors helped me disappear and fade into the background, but it was hard to fade into my body when I was standing next to Jannipp. Even sitting next to her called men's attention to me. I was with her, so I must be like her, even with my drab T-shirts and torn jeans.

"You look so hot," she told me the first time I put on a black miniskirt and the heels she tossed at me from her own closet. She was skinnier than me, a long line of dark brown skin and bones, so her clothing fit me snugly, accentuating the curves I often muted with loose clothing.

"I don't want to look hot," I mumbled, my shoulders sinking into my chest. "It doesn't feel good. It's not me."

"Of course not," she squealed. "Not yet. But the more you dress yourself up, the better you'll feel about yourself, and the more confident you'll be."

I nodded, half-believing her. It was fun at first, finding myself at the center of the male gaze, but only at first. Eventually, the eyes my body collected became heavy and overbearing. They didn't belong to young boys my age—which I was okay with. I could handle nineteen or twenty-year-old eyes. But I wasn't okay with the fifty-year-old eyes, the toothy grins, the pictures I saw of myself reflected in the drowsy orbs of adult male eyes. The whistles. The roving leers. I wanted to throw up, all the time.

I had a date one night with a Greek boy I met during one of my shifts at the jeans store. Jannipp helped me get ready for the date by lending me her black miniskirt, low black heels, and a pink silk shirt with frilly sleeves. I loved the frilly sleeves the most. They reminded me of Victorian clothing, the way the sleeves hugged the arm and then flowed out like blossoming flowers. I went to work this way, and when my female manager saw me, she pulled me off the floor and placed me at the entrance of the store.

"Just make sure no one leaves without any unpurchased items," she told me. It was common for her to replace our security guard with a floor seller, but it had never been me before. I was small and quiet, and the girls that she usually put by the entrance for this position were big-boned and big-mouthed. The kind of girls who would get into someone's face if they caught them stealing. That wasn't me. I was more comfortable being on the floor, folding shirts and jeans and tidying up the aisles, hiding in the stockroom when it got too crowded or loud for me.

It took me a minute to realize that she had placed me there as eye candy, a role I was not used to playing in any part of my life, let alone at work. Eyes penetrated me, going past the layers of my clothes, burning the skin that hid beneath. Male eyes. Eyes that made me feel dirty and slutty and fixed to their fantasies of sex. Young eyes and old eyes and all eyes in between that stripped me and laid me bare on the ground without me present.

A group of young men walked past me, their eyes searing me like a slab of meat, branding me with the sex they saw in me.

"You have a great future behind you," one of them piped up.

"Fuck you!" I flung the words at him, wanting to hurt him back, to cut him down to pieces I felt myself being torn into.

They only laughed. My insides burned, heat rising to my cheeks, inside my mouth, my eyes.

"I can't do this," I told my boss when she came to check up on me. "Please let me work in the stockroom tonight."

She heaved a sigh and pointed to the back of the store. I forced myself not to run into its black depths, prying items out of sealed boxes, making order out of chaos.

My next job, one in which I was hired to count the money that came from television and phone rentals in major hospitals from New York to New Jersey, was no better. On the first day at work, I was reproached by my immediate manager because I came in dressed in black slacks.

"Didn't you hear what I said to you on the phone yesterday?" His eyes disavowed me as a renegade, breaking rules that were articulated and inherent in my offer of employment.

"Honestly, I was so excited to get a call, I didn't really hear anything more than 'you start tomorrow.'" That was the truth. I was a rule follower. If he said I couldn't wear pants, then I wouldn't have. I had nothing to prove. I needed the money to pay for college, and this was all I cared about at this point.

I watched Steve wrestle with the idea that I was telling the truth, that I hadn't really heard him. He sighed, and I relaxed with the knowledge that I would be given a second chance to prove myself.

"Our owner is Orthodox Jewish," he explained to me. "He believes that women should wear skirts or dresses. Only men wear pants. So can I count on you to dress appropriately tomorrow?"

I nodded, thankful for his generosity. I would wear skirts for this job. What choice did I have? It was a job and I had nothing else to help me pay for school.

Of course, they didn't care what kind of skirt I wore as long as they were skirts. Jannipp at this time gave me a purple spandex tank dress that fit me perfectly, hugging my rounded breasts and butt, my ribcage, and flat stomach. I was allowed to wear that, with or without a dressy sweater. No one said a word to me.

Wearing it on a Saturday, already dressed for a night out dancing at the clubs, earned me a hard, open palm slap on the ass by a young man at the company who didn't give me the time of day during the week.

"I'm sorry," he said, laughing. "It was there, so juicy. I had to do it." From a distance, I had appreciated his tall litheness, the fine blond hair on his head, the dimple on his chin, but after the slap, I saw who he was. How he treated girls. He hadn't even talked to me, had never said my name aloud, but it was quite acceptable to touch me, to put his hands on me. To remind me of my sex, to do what he wanted.

My boss, Steve, was no better. A husband to someone, a father to two boys who would one day look up to and model him, he dropped pens and asked me to pick them up for him.

"While you're down there," he smiled at me, not finishing the sentence.

When I took lunch orders, going from manager to manager and asking what they were in the mood to eat that day, a few of them responded with, "I want to eat some Greek today." Wink. Wink.

When I asked Steve for a letter of recommendation for a school program I wanted to join at Queens College, he wrote one for me, commenting on my shapely figure, being a sexy asset to the office, a pleasure to look at and be near. He let me read it, and when he didn't get the response he expected—an appreciative grin? laughter? a meek giggle?—he grabbed the letter from me and tore it to shreds.

I stood in front of his desk with my eyebrows twisted into knots and my mouth slack with confusion.

"It's a joke," he informed me. "You got that, right? I'm just playing with you. Here's the one you need for school." He passed me the correct letter in an envelope, hoping it would ease the stiffness that bore into my spine, forcing me to stand before him with a thick lump in my throat.

When I left this job, I worked for another man, the owner of a pharmaceutical wholesale company who called me to his office and unzipped his pants.

"I'm joking, baby," he laughed at me. "Go get me some coffee, will you?" I screwed up his order for days until he stopped asking me into his office or to get his coffee.

I couldn't escape these men, their eyes, their lewd mouths reminding me that I was only good for one thing all the while knowing I was going to school to get my teaching license. They only saw a twenty-something girl without the power to stand up to them, to fend for herself, reminding me more and more of the helplessness that emanated from the tainted pores of my childhood spent with Kristos, a man destined to teach me how to be a woman, the kind of woman who provided him with money and social clout.

They were all Kristos, and they came into my life at various times of my development as a girl, teaching me the cost of being a female.

When I threw myself into dating, it was with the hope that I would find love, and with it, a coupling that would make me undesirable to other men, protect me from them. But dating was another cesspool of disappointment, reminding me that my biology was my destiny, and that who I was as a person was unnecessary to what they wanted from me and believed they deserved. I asserted myself into their desires—refusing to be shut out of them—until I was too exhausted from the struggle it took to make them remember my name.

I kissed a lot of guys, dated a slew of them, but I didn't have sex with any of them. How long I went out with them, how far I let them get, that was all up to me. I was in control. And to ensure that roving hands and fingers didn't slip from an over-the-jeans caress to touching skin, I developed my own chastity belt, my warrior garb. There were no more dresses and skirts for me in my early twenties when dating took over my free time between school and work.

I bought myself onesies, tank tops, and shirts that snapped at the crotch. No access-zone shirts, I used to call them. I had one in velvet green, one in maroon, and a few in black and brown, and I put them on under tight jeans that showed off my slim and curvy figure, further concealed by red-and-white checkered flannel shirts that remained unbuttoned. To seal the deal, I put my small feet in black Timberland boots.

This ensemble made me feel tough, strong, in control of myself and my body. I could tussle in the back seat of a car with a boy, but my warrior clothes put the needed distance between us and empowered me to say no and mean it. And when they didn't stop, I turned cold and stiff in their hands, my mouth closed, eyes threatening them to defy me.

It worked. All of it. And those who only wanted sex from me disappeared from my life while those who were more patient dragged their feet a bit, hoping I would change my mind. I didn't. It was all a game. And the rules of this game had been taught to me by the men in my life. My teachers. Kristos. My father. Mr. Schwartz. Steve. And Stewart, the next boss who unzipped his pants for me and demanded I fetch his coffee.

It all stopped when I met Richard. When he came into my life, I was tired and lonely, and he waited an entire year and a half for me to be ready to have sex with him. It took me that long to trust him, to trust him with my body, my sex.

He gave me a home that could contain my heart, my sexuality, my own loving nature. His own experiences with loss and parental chaos made me feel understood and accepted, despite my anxieties, my traumas. He understood my pain, and he named feelings I didn't have names for. He even called me Marina long before I took back my name in front of Ann, just to fuck with her for taking away what was mine and should never have been taken from me in the first place. That is how loyal he was, how good and true and loving. In his arms, I was cared for and loved. Even protected.

How could I not fall in love with him? He was everything I was looking for and hoping I would find. He was what I needed to feel safe enough to love him back, to surrender my body and its fears to him, all the way through, past its histories and defenses.

He was home. Family. Love.

Until he wasn't.

DODGING TRIGGERS

My adoptive mother had a heart attack right before the pandemic hit. She was on the subway headed home from Manhattan, and as she walked up the steps on the Elmhurst stop where she lives, she collapsed.

"I didn't collapse or pass out," she corrected me many times.

"What would you call it?" I asked, raising my bushy eyebrows at her, a smile playing at my lips. Of course, she didn't collapse. She was always in control.

"I felt weak, my heart was palpitating, so I lay down on the ground to avoid passing out."

A young woman took care of her by helping her up, guiding her out of the subway to the main street, and ordering an Uber to take my mother to the ER. When she asked my mother if there was anyone she could call for her, my mother said, "Richard, my son-in-law."

"I didn't want to bother you," she explained later. "You're so busy with school and work and the children. I don't want to be a burden." But I knew better. She was avoiding me the same way I avoided her. Richard was our proxy, our safe go-between.

Although there was a time my mother did not like Richard and referred to him as a "talker," refusing to say his name aloud until the day we were married, she and Richard became friends. And roommates.

Two years after Richard lost his job, the only trading firm that would take a chance on him was in Manhattan. It made sense for him, while working in New York, to stay with my mother who, at eighty-five years of age, needed someone to watch out for her. He stayed with her for eight months until she finally told him to leave. He had overstayed his welcome. My mother was used to living alone, having her space to herself with no one to bother her. If she wanted company, she went to lunch in the city with the Greek Club or the Japanese Club, or took crafting classes for seniors at Hunter College or the local senior citizens' center. She was a loner, but she liked talking to people, making temporary friends she would see only once or twice a month, and at her discretion.

As much as she complained about Richard because he cleaned her kitchen counters, rewashed her utensils, and solved all the *Wheel of Fortune* puzzles before she did, I also knew that she liked having him around. He was company, a man who enjoyed being around old people and knew how to listen to them, humor them, let them have their say.

"He cheats at *Jeopardy*," she told me many times, her voice shaking with laughter and ending with a snort.

"I know," I replied over the phone. "I couldn't understand how he always beat me at Scrabble, and eventually, I realized that while my eyes were buried in the dictionary looking for words to win, he was stealing the letters from the box that would yield him the most points. This is why we don't like to play games with him at home. He cheats all the time."

They watched *Jeopardy* and *Wheel of Fortune* every night after dinner, and when he came to North Carolina on the weekends to stay with us, she called him to ensure he'd made it home all right.

I wasn't hurt by their friendship, their relationship. At first. He had somewhere to stay for free while he was working in New York, and she had someone to keep an eye on her in case she fell or had a stroke or a heart attack or whatever else ambushes older people her age. Like all the things that are too hard for me to deal with, I passed the care of my mother on to him. And he assumed the burden without question.

The evening she had her first heart attack, Richard was driving back to North Carolina from Queens. It took him twelve hours, and just as he laid his body down on the living room couch to relax after dinner, his phone rang.

"Your mother had a heart attack," he told me when he got off the phone with the young girl who had called an Uber to take my mother to Elmhurst Hospital.

"You have to go back," I told him without thinking. "I'm teaching on Monday. I can't go to New York and cancel my classes. But you have to be back in New York anyway for work, so it makes sense that you go."

I was keenly aware of my body, the brittle bones inside me quaking with fear, thoughts running wild in my head with the speed and chaos of unbridled horses let loose in an open field after someone fired a bullet into the wind. They collided and pushed against each other for momentum, their legs, long and powerful, propelling them forward and away from the danger they perceived.

"You should go," he told me. "She's *your* mother."

"She didn't call *me*," I pointed out to him, half-smiling. Yes, it bothered me, but I was used to her rejections. Her refusal to walk me down the aisle on the day of my wedding. Another refusal to attend Joseph's baptismal. The time she told Richard he would make a great mother, as I lay in a hospital bed having just given birth to my son. The time she told me I wasn't in her will, but I was the executor, so I would know what she was not leaving me. The time she was looking at a Christmas family picture — my family's picture — and wanted to know who the fat woman in the portrait was. Of course, it was me. Who else would the woman in the snapshot with my husband and children be?

Richard became the only human bridge that kept me and my mother connected. If it weren't for him driving us to New York for Thanksgiving with his family or to my book reading at the feminist bookstore in the city, I would not have made it back to New York. These are my failings, my fear of traveling alone, driving long distances alone, seeing my mother alone, without Richard as my driver, my leader, my crutch. I am crippled with anxieties, and a part of me knows that, without Richard in my life, doing for me all the things that paralyze me, I would melt into the desperation that feeds on my insides and disappear from life altogether.

"I can't go," I repeated. "It doesn't make sense. I have to work. I would have to fly, and we don't have money for that. I wouldn't have a car to take her home from the hospital when they release her. You would drive and have a car. Plus, I don't know the city anymore or its transportation system. I'd get lost on the subway. You know it better. It makes more sense for you to go."

Let's not forget my fear of driving in the city or in Queens. I learned how to drive there and forced myself to drive to Manhattan once a month so I could control my fear. My little white Acura Integra and I conquered the Long Island Expressway, the Belt Parkway, the 59th Street Bridge that led to the city, the Brooklyn Bridge, and the Grand Central Parkway. But having been away from city driving for the past twelve years, I had become timid, anxious at the idea of driving in chaos, preferring the slow, tepid, easy two-lane roads that have nurtured and lulled me back to safety in Cary, North Carolina.

Richard needed to be at work on Monday, anyway, I repeated inside my head, the guilt of shirking my daughterly responsibilities gnawing on my wrist bone like an annoying mosquito feeding on the cowardice circulating in my blood.

He packed his backpack with underwear and a few outfits for work, got into his car, and drove toward the highway that led him back to New York. I called my childhood friend Jody and asked her to go to the hospital to spend some time with my mom. I couldn't be there, but I didn't want her to be alone while she waited for Richard to arrive. I didn't want to be there for oh, so many reasons that I am still ironing out, but the inconveniences to my life were the only excuses I could articulate at the time.

The hospital kept her over the weekend and sent her home on Monday with heart medication. Richard went to work during the day and stayed with her in the evenings. After a week, she seemed fine, and he returned home to us.

But the same thing happened again. He was in Virginia this time, three hours away from our home, when my mother called Richard from the hospital. Not me. Him again. She went to the hospital to ask them to change her medication, which was making her fingers numb and her thoughts fuzzy. But once they connected her to an EKG and saw that her heart was in cardiac arrest, they admitted her. She had been walking around with a defective heart.

It was the first week of December, and they kept her for an entire week.

"You have to come," Richard told me. "They don't think she'll make it. The doctor said you should come."

I made the arrangements. I submitted my grades, completed my final exams for my PhD classes early, made sure my daughter would spend the weekend with a friend from school, and put my trust in my son that he would drive to and from school that Friday without getting into an accident. There would be no one to help him since I would be on a flight to New York, and Richard would be on his way back from New York and wouldn't arrive until two or three in the morning.

I went straight from JFK airport to Elmhurst Hospital, the

traffic a harsh, impatient reminder of why I had left New York in the first place. It takes two hours to get anywhere in the city with all the congestion, the cars, the people filling every crevice of space available to the human eye. There is no corner untouched by pollution, debris, human form, or saliva spewed from the mouths of people who want to leave evidence of their existence behind, even if it is in the scrapes and cracks of the cemented pavement upon which we trample.

When I arrived at my mother's hospital room, I found her sitting upright in a chair, tucked into her black winter jacket, looking frail and thinner than the last time I'd seen her the previous Christmas, her legs propped onto her bed. I sat in the chair opposite her, trying not to wake her, and took her in.

When I see her now, in her old age, I don't see the woman who failed to give me what I needed. I mean, all of that is there, always, like a little child holding a grudge, nudging me not to forget, not to forgive, not to be blinded by the generosity she never showed me when I was younger.

Her wallet is open now, as she sends me bonds for school, for lawn services, for trips, for the kids. Growing up, I fended for myself. I worked two jobs while going to school and paid for my own tuition, which she refused to help me pay unless I came home every day at eight in the evening and obeyed her every wish. But now that I had children and no longer needed her assistance, her generosity was endless.

Other forms of generosity include questions like "How is your sister?" when I returned from a trip to Greece last summer, wanting my brother and sister to finally meet my children outside of Facebook and photographs sent to their homes each Christmas.

"She's fine," I responded and left it at that.

I can't give her more. I can't offer up my family to her now that she pretends to care. When I was little, she acted as if they didn't exist, changed my name, and called me a liar whenever I spoke about my childhood, the violence, the depravity of the life that ran in my thoughts like a movie reel without an end. And the thing is, as an adult, I want to tell her about my family. But my tongue is stuck in my mouth, and the words remain lodged behind my tongue, glued to the roof of my mouth.

She took my voice away, and every time I am near her, I become mute.

"You don't have much more to tell me?" she asks. I shake my head.

"It was good seeing them. Nothing more to tell." We both drop the subject, and she resumes her advice about making pastitsio, Greek pasta with meat sauce, and how to keep mixing the milk for the béchamel sauce or else it sticks to the bottom of the pan and browns.

I am quiet in her presence. The kind of quiet I have learned works well with personalities larger than my own, personalities that command first place, first rights, and constant wins.

Hers. And Richard's.

They are stronger, not physically, but energetically, and they impose themselves on those of us who don't have the energy to fight back. They're not abusive or mean, although they could be. But they want the last word. They want to know they are right. And they find people like me, non-confrontational people who bow down when conflict assumes their space, their hard-won desire for peace. It's manipulation, a skill that I have not mastered and do not want to.

Ann taught me to back down, to resist conflict by giving in to it. *It doesn't matter what I say*, I used to remind myself. *Let her talk. Let her have the last word. Let her think she has won. Why struggle?*

Fighting her as a child never got me anything except months of silence, wherein she passed me in the narrow hallway of our small apartment without touching me, without seeing me, without a word. Those silences were awful, painful for me. And when I could no longer stand to wake up feeling like the ghost she made me, I pleaded for her eyes to bathe in me, her voice to touch me, even while her hands refused to grab my own or squeeze my shoulders or glide over my stringy, unbrushed hair.

"I'm sorry. It's all my fault. I won't do it again," I broke the silence. I lost the fight.

"What won't you do again?" she asked me, looking down at me, her chin cocked over my head with cold authority.

"I won't be rude. I won't talk back. I'll be respectful." I listed my failings, promising obedience, which is what she had wanted from me since the beginning. Peace in her home meant obedience.

But the truth is, I never believed it. I hadn't been rude, and a part of me believed that I needed to speak my truth. It was ridiculous to silence a child. Unforgivable to tell her that her birth family did not exist. She wanted me to lie about myself, to make sure no one knew that I had been adopted by her. Not even my friends could know, and as soon as I made a new friend, her first question was always, "Have you told her?

"Told her what?" I asked, playing dumb.

"That you're adopted. That I'm not your real mother."

"Not yet," I answered openly. "Maybe if we get closer. If it lasts."

"Well, I don't want you talking to anyone about me. Behind my back," she said after a while.

"I wouldn't be talking about you," I explained. "I would be talking about me."

Her secret was my secret, too. Except I wasn't ashamed of being adopted. And I didn't care who knew. But for some reason, this was my mother's biggest secret, a shameful one that I didn't have the skills to tap into, to understand. And today, I simply don't care. The damage has been done.

I am damaged, still finding it hard to locate the language I need to convey my truest feelings, horrified that if I put my truth out on the table that sits between me and someone else, they won't love me or care for me anymore. The truth changes everything, so I keep it locked in the chest beneath my rib cage, taking two Tums a day to alleviate the heartburn that remains lodged there, spasming violently at the prospect of having my words exhumed.

Sitting five feet away from my mother, her head cocked to the side, snoring into the lapels of her jacket in her hospital room, these thoughts did not ruminate or nudge or scream for attention. I was only aware of her fragility, of the reality that this could be the end—of her, of her and me, that with her death would come the death of this heavy guilt that hovers about me like a fog whenever I move. Guilt that I have failed her. That I haven't lived up to her expectations. That I haven't forgiven her. Her death would give me the reprieve I need to breathe aloud as myself for the very first time without the grim shadow of her mothering looming over me. It's either her death or my death. All or nothing.

But it wasn't her time. It was Saturday, and the night before, the doctors had given her digoxin, a miracle heart drug that completely changed the rules of her congestive heart failure. Overnight, she was able to get out of her bed without assistance, eat her food, and open her eyes wide. Her thoughts were clear, and she did not sink into sleep like a rock falling to the bottom of the pool, hard and weighty.

When she opened her eyes and saw me sitting there, opposite her, she didn't recognize me at first.

"It's me," I smiled at her. "Marina."

It was awkward telling her my name. I always want to revert to the name she gave me when she adopted me at the age of eight, Kathryn. I feel guilty for taking back my birth name, so I don't bring it up. She and I never had a conversation about it. Why I did it. What it meant to have my name taken away from me.

I was Marina again after twenty-five years of wearing the

wrong name over my skin and loathing myself for it. Richard referred to me as Marina when he spoke to her, and eventually, she picked up the information and began calling me Marina as well. But every time her mouth says *Marina*, we both hear the awkwardness that lies beneath the sound, all the unuttered words that breathe and whisper between us, dancing in frantic circles around the name, bouncing off each other in chaotic spurts, popping their heads up and down for attention, wanting to be heard, to be uttered, which my mother and I will not do.

It's always like that between us, whether we are on the phone or face-to-face. We skirt around heavy topics like my childhood, my name, my trauma, her mismothering of me, and we talk about the weather instead. Or the kids. Or how to bake *koulouri*, the Greek Easter bread. Or how she wishes Richard would return to school so he could get a decent job in North Carolina instead of driving to New York every week, which must be hard on us all.

I closed the distance between the visitor's chair and where she sat on the other side of her bed, hugging her, noting the thinness of her upper arms when I clasped her, the fragility of her fingers as they trembled when she raised them to wipe a strand of white hair from her eyes. Eyes that used to cast me in coldness, called me a liar, and undressed me in search of evidence of sex and drugs and alcohol now radiated with pleasure to find me at the hospital, waiting for her to awaken.

I walked back to my chair, the length of her hospital bed situated between us like a thick layer of an ironclad partition for protection. My protection. Sitting back, I forced a smile at her, small and thin, to cover up the discomfort I felt, being alone with her in a room without much to say. Without Richard standing beside me to lighten the loaded space between us with levity and jokes, filling in the silences with words he had no trouble mustering up for surface conversations that required no depth or honesty.

I sat. And I waited for the nurses to tell me I could take her home when all I wanted to do was run in the opposite direction. Back to my home. My family. Where I was safe and hidden from her.

MOMMY DEAREST

My mother's home is currently a condo one block away from the house I grew up in. Seven steps lead from the main floor containing the living room and kitchen to a master bedroom connected to a tiny bathroom; a small room she uses as her office, sewing room, and television-watching space; and a guest bathroom with a full bath.

Watching her take those seven steps, one at a time, after her second heart attack, her thin knuckles clinging to the banister, was like watching a turtle cross the street, impatient car owners honking their horns, letting it know their time is more valuable than one hard-shelled turtle. As I do with the turtles or a family of geese crossing intersections in front of my car back home, I guarded her slow progress. I stood behind her, took a step forward each time she did, my hands braced to catch her if she lost her balance.

Once she reached the top level, I took a deep breath. She shuffled into her room. I helped her onto her bed, and she fell asleep. Back in the living room, I took out her pills and placed them in a line across the surface of her Chinese cabinet, pink blossoms running like loose vines along the red lacquer chinoiserie, in the order she was required to take them. There were eight bottles, and she was expected to take twelve pills a day.

"I'm a drug addict now," she told me, shaking her head, the white curls of her hair bouncing against her gaunt cheeks.

I was moved by her fragility. I had never known her in this weak, slow, aged body. She was always a force to be reckoned with, her outer shell solid and sure of itself set against the hunched and timid one belonging to me. That still belongs to me. Afraid of breathing too much lest the act take up too much space needed by someone more worthy. More significant. Like her.

I understood that losing control of her body, her independence, was the greatest strain in her nineties. She must take drugs all the time now, every day, for the rest of the time remaining and belonging to her. She may soon need a nurse to care for her, even live with her. Or she may have to go to a nursing home. She wants none of these options. She wants to live in her home until the day her body shuts down and she leaves it all behind.

I made her eggs and toast and went to the store for vegetables and bread. I didn't mind shopping for her. I didn't mind cooking for her. I didn't mind taking care of her. Helping her up and down the seven steps. Making sure she took her pills and fetching her water. Taking care of others is what I do. I have done it for nineteen years, with my own kids. Feeding them. Taking them to the doctor. Keeping track of their medication when they have been sick. I never minded being the caregiver to them, and I didn't mind this part of being with my mother.

I minded the other stuff.

I minded sitting down next to her to watch British detective shows, the volume so high it vibrated across my skin and felt like a thousand needle pricks all at once.

I minded sitting opposite her as she ate, watching dregs of her meal rest on her upper lip, hearing the swishing sounds of her food being chewed and smashed, mixing with the saliva in her mouth.

I minded the way she asked me a question, and when I answered her, she couldn't hear me, so I repeated myself, yelling so she could grasp my words. Her hearing was weak and talking to her—having to yell everything, even a simple no or yes or I don't know—was like scraping my teeth against gravel. That painful. That aggravating.

I minded eating with her utensils and finding hardened food she had failed to wash off because her eyesight was diminishing or sipping coffee from her cup and seeing leftover particles from a meal in my drink.

I minded these because they made my stomach turn, my throat lodging itself shut to any future meals at her home. I lost four pounds in five days because I could not eat with her.

I minded when she came to the couch, where I slept and made my home, watching Netflix for a breather away from her, for a moment of quiet I only find in myself, when I could feel the muscles beneath me relax, my jaw loosen from its locked position, and sat beside me, a smile pressed against her thin lips. I watched her from a distance, though she was a breath's space from me, and I could feel my limbs renouncing her closeness, my back hugging the arm of the couch for support, my knees glued together to keep them from—from what?

I don't know. My whole body was like a taut wire, an over-wound violin string ready to pop and spring apart from its coil at the slightest stroke of a finger.

She asked questions, one after the other, being pleasant, but I was far away from her. Aware of the tension in my bones, I heard a hum in my ears, void of any other sounds around me. I returned my answers with simple phrases. *Yes. No. Maybe. I don't know.* This was all I could muster around her. The only words I could yell at her. And when she reached out to touch me, I warned my arm not to pull back. I tensed like a metal rod neither fire nor God could yield or bend.

This is on you, I told myself. *Don't hurt her. Don't reject her.* I sat still, nodding my head, trying to quiet the screams inside me, forcing myself to be present, so she could not see I was not there, that I did not want to be there. With her.

After five days, I couldn't take it anymore. I booked us tickets with Amtrak, ordered an Uber to Central Station, and held her elbow as she shuffled to the gate leading us home. My home. My kids. To Richard, who would take over the charge of her, humor her while I disappeared into myself again—where my body quietly abides, happy and free.

Until when? Until it no longer has to, I think. That's what I wait for. For the end. Its inevitability is still a comfort to me.

In my home, I slept in my bed. I cooked in my kitchen, where the dishes and utensils and pots and pans had been washed until there was no evidence of food or dirt on them. Everything entering my mouth was clean and pure, and I didn't get sick to my stomach when I was hungry or thirsty.

In my home, I had my kids, and I loved being with them, having them enter the spaces of my existence to remind me I am wanted, needed, and loved. They didn't make my body retreat or my limbs tense with discomfort. For them, with them, I was open and happy, and laughter came easily.

At home, I had my car, and when I felt too stifled by my mother's presence, or Richard's, or anyone's, I got into it and drove to freedom. The movies. A coffee shop. The mall. The Hemlock Bluffs trails I used to take the kids to when they were little, where it can take me up to an hour to trudge through leaves and mulch from the entrance into the thick of the woods and then back again, the only noise coming from the conversations taking place in my head, too disruptive, too terrible to be given license to exit as actual words, actual sounds with consequences.

Richard made a mock bedroom for her in the piano room, laying an air mattress on the floor and positioning my bookcase in front of it to give her a semblance of privacy since there are no doors in the room. He put the smaller bookcase next to the bed so she could rest and charge her phone on it, lay her glasses and whatever book she was reading on it, within reach.

My mother doesn't like navigating spaces in which she is not the boss, not in control. Richard and I took turns cooking. She didn't like my cooking, commented on there not being enough salt or pepper or spices in it. The chicken was too dry. Too overcooked. We humored her. Well, Richard humored her. The rest of us laughed it off politely.

My kids and I disappeared up the stairs and into the small quarters of our respective rooms. She could not follow us. There were too many stairs, and she had not regained her strength. I made an exorbitant number of plans for my daughter, Rena, that involved my being with her. At the movies and dinner with friends. At their home. At Defy Gravity, watching youthfulness bounce from one trampoline to the other without a care in the world. Richard was the only one who stayed downstairs with her, showing her how to use Netflix or Amazon Prime to stream her British mysteries, or how to increase the volume the kids and I could hear all the way upstairs, with our doors closed.

We went bowling for Richard's fiftieth birthday, and Richard and the kids let me win because they knew how much it would piss off Grandma. She forced a smile my daughter could see was fake and nodded her head, her eyebrows arched with disappointment that I won somehow. I didn't know how to explain to my children why my mother wanted me to fail—even in something as arbitrary and ridiculous as bowling. But they noticed her forced and false reactions toward me.

"You let her control you," my mother goaded Richard after three weeks of staying with us, when we were all tired of each other. "Do you do everything she tells you to do?"

This resulted from my ordering Chinese food for dinner one night. She didn't want Chinese. She wanted a calzone from the pizzeria. I was making too many decisions in my own home with my family, and she didn't like it. She wasn't used to seeing me in a position of power or authority.

I realized this a year earlier, when we went to New York for Thanksgiving. Richard's family throws big family celebrations at a farmhouse in Westchester, and this was the first time we'd joined them in years. We made sure to also visit my mother and take her out to dinner. After spending the day in the city, taking pictures by the Christmas tree in Rockefeller Center, and shopping for winter jackets for the kids, which my mother wanted to buy for them, we took the train back to Queens, starving. I recommended we stop at Forest Hills and eat there. My teen years had been spent in Forest Hills, hanging out with my friends at Pizzeria Uno, and later on, many of my dates took place along those avenues, a short walk from the train where I met them and then could head home once the date ended.

We found an Italian restaurant along Woodhaven Boulevard. My choice because I was hungry and tired, and my kids looked as exhausted as I felt, as hungry as I imagined, and I could walk no more. When we entered the restaurant, it was empty, and I told the waitress to sit us by the window. It began to snow, and I wanted the kids to watch the snow fall. She didn't like the restaurant. She didn't like the table I chose.

"I don't like this area. Let's sit elsewhere," she instructed the waitress without asking us.

"This is fine," I said, dismissing her resistance, having reached my fill with her complaints, her constant negation of my choices, like a leech clinging onto my leg, sucking at the nutrients I reserved for my children's needs. My kids were rolling their eyes, their fingers impatiently scrolling down the menu to see if they could find their favorites: chicken français for Joseph; chicken parmesan for Rena. They smashed buttered bread into their mouths as if they hadn't eaten in months. We just wanted to eat.

"You're bossy," she told me, eyeing me from across the table. "Is she always this bossy?" She turned her question to my kids, who shook their heads at her, but looked at me and rounded their eyes as if to say, *What the hell?*

"Do you always get your way?" she continued, and though I didn't drink, I ordered a large glass of pinot grigio to help me get through the next hour.

"The kids are hungry and want to eat. It doesn't matter where or what. They're starving," I told her, my eyes glued to the menu without really seeing any of the words popping out at me.

She couldn't stand to have me make any decisions affecting her that night, like where she would eat or where she could sit, and this became even more glaring when she spent three weeks in my home. A home I was comfortable being myself in, could move about with ease, my body fluid and confident in its motions, my voice assertive when telling the kids to practice the piano or take a shower, when telling Richard what I wanted for dinner or when we needed to leave by to get to our friends' home on time for dinner plans.

She spent Christmas and New Year's with my family, getting stronger and more resentful as each day passed. The last time she spent Christmas with us, my kids had been younger, maybe nine and five. She had stayed a week, which was too long. For both of us. I couldn't wait to drop her off at the airport back then, and she couldn't get out of my car fast enough. It was mutual. This time, she was stuck with us for three weeks, and after New Year's, when Richard returned to New York for work, she left with him, though she despised the idea of being in a car for twelve hours. The plan was for him to stay with her for the next week or so and see if she would need home care. Then he would go to his apartment in Staten Island.

Again, she was glad to leave, and I was glad to have her go. She did not belong with me or with my family. Visiting her one or two days a year was enough for all of us. But she did have the last word the night before she left, reminding me of my place.

"Don't take this personally, but I am going to change my will and make Richard my executor. I don't think you can manage my affairs." We were all in the kitchen, and I was on my way out the door to take Rena to the movies with her friend.

"If that's what you want." I let the hurt roll off my shoulders and smashed it with my foot when it fell on the floor. "It's your will. You should do what you're comfortable with. Gotta go. See you all later." I rushed out of the house, Rena at my heels, hoping my mother hadn't seen a trickle of hurt seeping out of my pores.

What made it even more painful was catching Richard fist-bumping the air when he heard her comment. The prospect of overseeing her money gave him financial relief. There was a time he would have stood up to her, told her off, defended me. But not now. Not anymore. Now we were in competition. I wanted her love. He wanted her money. He was winning.

Two days later, after she and Richard returned to New York and her home, I called to make sure they made it home all right.

"It's very good to be home again," she told me, her voice slightly winded from having to descend the stairs to reach the phone in her kitchen.

"I bet. I would hate to be away from my home all this time."

"What did you say?" she yelled into the phone. "I can't hear well. You'll have to speak slower."

"Nothing. Good. I'm glad you're feeling stronger." I repeated my words slowly, loudly, so she could hear.

Pause.

"I hope you don't mind," she began. "But since you're so busy with the kids and work, I thought it would be better if I put Richard down as my emergency contact. This way, if anything happens, they will call him first. You'll be second, of course," she added, as if being second should make me feel better about not being first.

I sighed, a shrill sound of surrender escaping my nose, my eyes stinging from her rejection.

"If that's what you want," I returned, trying to exude nonchalance as if it is in my nature.

"Do you want to talk to Richard?" she asked, and when I told her no, I would talk to him later, we both hung up.

When Richard returned a week later, I argued with him relentlessly. Every time he called her, or she called him, it felt as if he were cheating on me. To make matters worse, he began talking with her on the phone in the garage, rolling back and forth on the rocking chair we'd used to nurse and lull our two children to sleep when they were younger. It was a secret relationship, a private conversation that excluded me altogether. They began calling each other without my knowing about it.

"I want you to stop taking her calls," I demanded several times.

"That makes no sense. You're being hysterical. Look at you." His voice was calm, which I hated. He did this whenever I became angry. But when he showed anger, punching the keys on his computer, denting our refrigerator or pantry door with his knuckles, grunting and fuming at the stock market for not going his way, God forbid I should call him hysterical or emotional.

"I'm your family. Not her. Your loyalty is to me. If she doesn't want me in her life, then you should have nothing to do with her, either." I spoke as calmly as I could muster, controlling my tone, my voice, trying in earnest to make him understand this was the time to show me he loved me. Twenty years ago, he had chosen me. He'd been rude to my mother, put her in her place to show me he still saw me in the shadows she draped all over me as if my body were a corpse in a casket, forgotten and decayed.

"Marina, you know why I'm doing this. She's leaving the kids money. They'll be taken care of in ways we can't afford. We're broke. We're in debt. Be practical."

"I don't want to use her," I retorted. "I don't want her money. I want nothing from her, and you need to stop calling her." By calling her, he was keeping her in my life when I wanted nothing more to do with Ann.

Every time I spoke to her, she insulted me, hurt me, reminded me of all the ways I had failed as a daughter, and now as a wife and mother. My children were too quiet because I traumatized them. Joseph, my son, was gay because I traumatized him. Talking to her left me shrinking with shame and trepidation. I couldn't escape her, and the only way I knew to keep her from hurting me was to not talk to her. To withdraw myself from her attentions.

But Richard insisted he was only keeping ties with her to ensure she would leave her money to our kids. Even though I was not in her will, our kids were. Like all her digs, this one hurt as well, slicing into the numb facade I pretended to recoil into for protection. But all my pretenses were for nothing. She made her digs, and they never failed to sting. I constructed an outer shell for protection from her hurts, but I assembled it out of sticks and pebbles with old, crusted glue that wasn't strong enough to withstand her verbal affronts.

Her choice of Richard as her executor instead of me made me tremble with anxiety and rejection. She knew it would. And even though Richard knew why she was doing it, he cared more about getting her money than about my feelings. He continued to talk to her, maintained a relationship with her that I repeatedly asked him to end. For me. But he didn't care, and I suppose that, for the first time, I truly believed I was no longer a priority for him. He only cared about the money and our kids. I was an afterthought, if that.

"I never took money from her," I reminded him. "I paid for my undergraduate and graduate degrees without her help. Our kids can get loans or pay for their school by working, just like we did. We don't need her money. Not at this cost. She's rejecting me again and again, and you're telling her it's okay to do it. She thinks she can have you without me, my kids without me, and that is not okay. She can't go around me as if I don't exist, and you're letting her do just that."

Voicing my concerns to him was exhausting. I felt like a child again, unable to master the language required to shift someone's position, this time, my husband's. I should not have to work so hard to be shown love and loyalty, and it made me question my inability to do so. What was wrong with me that everyone who claimed to love me chose their own needs over mine?

"You sound like a jealous girlfriend," he said, laughing. It reminded me of the way he'd pumped his fist in the air when he heard her tell me she wanted him to be the executor of her will.

"None of this is funny," I said to him, hoping the coldness in my voice would bring him back to me. The guy who had chosen me once. The one who would now choose me all over again. Over my mother. Over her money.

"Look, all of this will fade into nothing. She wanted to have her say. To hurt you. She did. Don't give her all this power over you."

"You're giving her power over me," I pointed out. "You're letting her push me into the corner of my own family by continuing to be her friend, to call her, to act as if nothing has happened between me and her."

"I'm not doing anything to you. This is all you. Stop playing the victim."

I walked away from him then, slammed the door to our master bathroom, and wept into my empty hands. My body trembled with shame, guilt, and self-reproach.

I wanted to blow everything up, dismantle it from the inside, my fingernail itching to pull the trigger that would violently pop the dysfunctional bubble they believed could exist without me.

My mother had no one. But because of me, she had access to

grandchildren, a family, and Richard—who stayed with her when he was in New York, spent time with her, played *Wheel of Fortune*, and humored her. She couldn't have him without me around. She couldn't have grandchildren or anyone to care for her, take care of her end-of-life wishes, clear out her apartment. She'd be alone without me.

And Richard? He wouldn't have access to her money without me. The kids would, but not him. They both needed me, but they acted like I was a sidepiece, an irrelevant pawn in their let's-pretend-we-care-about-each-other game. And I loathe games. I don't play them. Never have. I felt used and insignificant in my own life, shoved into the corner and told to be nice and quiet, like a good little girl, while the adults in my circle played their adult games.

I was alone, dismissed by the two people who were supposed to care for me. And the only one who saw me in the muck that had become my life, who cared enough to reach out to me, was not even an adult.

"Mom," Joseph began the next day as I drove him to Chapel Hill for a program initiative geared toward high school students interested in pursuing medicine. "I don't need Grandma's money. I can pay for school with loans."

"Thanks, honey. I'm sorry you had to hear all that. I was just upset."

"You know," he began again after a brief pause. "If you want to leave Dad, then do it. Don't stay with him because of me and Rena. We'll be fine. You need to do what's best for you."

I peeled my eyes from the road to sneak a look at him. He was seventeen then, smart and beautiful, a soulful kid who knows more than he says, who holds his thoughts close to his chest, so they don't run away from him, be overtaken by the wrong people, those who won't understand him.

It's hard to have honest talks with my kids. I want to be open with them, to tell them the truth, but I have to be careful. There are some things I can't tell them. Like the fact that I am and have been unhappy. That I often fantasize about tearing down the house I live in and starting anew, taking him and Rena with me. But how do you say this to your kids, unfasten them from all they know and have known? From their roots and the security I have worked so hard to give them?

I can't. It is the hardest thing to do, living in this duality where the choices are sacrificing myself or sacrificing my kids. For a long time, for over a decade, I chose to sacrifice myself—all the way. I know what it's like to be collateral damage in the lives of adults who make all the decisions, right or wrong. To be the last one chosen because I was the child. That adults' needs superseded my own was the earliest and most constant lesson taught to me. I wouldn't do it to them. Even if it killed me.

"Thanks, Joseph. It means a lot to me, but I don't want you to worry about me. It's my job to worry about you. Okay?" He nodded.

"I love you so much," I added a few seconds later, hoping my words would exude light on the heaviness resting on his already sloped shoulders. Hoping my choices, my own silences and fears, had not forced this excess weight onto him.

"I love you, too," he told me, inserting his AirPods back in his ears, his eyes closed, shutting out the world and the mother whose fears of failure and failing others stunted her growth and ability to unload the weight of her un-choices and un-decisions.

Five days later, I was back in therapy, the only place I could give voice to words and desires growing like unbridled weeds all around me, deprived of sun and water, winding about my bones and muscles, gripping me with vice-like precision as they searched for a way out of my body, deeply fractured and tense with misgivings.

PART III

Marina, The Unsexed,
Mother and Wife

THE FIRST TIME

I don't remember the first time I had sex.

I know Richard was my first. I was twenty-five when I moved in with him, and I was still a virgin.

But I don't remember the first time we went all the way. Any of it. The day. The moment. The month. Or the details. Which is strange, considering I waited so long to have sex. So long to find him, love him. So long before it was okay for me to have sex without feeling like the dirty and debased whore Ann deemed me when I was just eleven years old.

When I first met Richard, at a small bar in Queens, I was twenty-three. He liked me though I wore my onesies, my jeans, and my combat boots. I wasn't wearing the flannel shirt over my onesie the night we met, and he says it was my shapely butt that caught his attention first. He came near me to get a glimpse of my face and liked the way my hair fell into my eyes, my wide-rimmed glasses that told him I was a nerd, and the way the red-brown lipstick outlined my thin lips and highlighted my toothy grin, when I did grin.

He was impressed with me because I didn't care that he was between jobs.

"Why would it matter?" I asked him. "It's not like I'm marrying you. I'm only getting to know you."

"Most girls care," he pointed out.

"That's stupid." I dismissed his concern.

I knew I had fallen in love with him when I no longer wanted to kiss other boys. It took me a while to get there, but when I did, I knew it would be okay for Richard to be the last boy I would ever kiss. I was looking for him — someone like him — and when I was close enough to him and felt I could trust him with myself, I told him about my birth mother, my adoptive mother, about the corruptive sex in my childhood, my need for unconditional love, and my unwillingness to have sex until I felt safe and loved.

I was still a virgin when I met him. Having never had control over any other parts of my life — or over the people who had control over me — when I had sex and with whom was the one thing I could control.

Unlike all the other boys I kissed before him, he waited for me. He waited until I was ready, which took almost two years. He waited for me to catch up, to feel loved, invested in, nurtured into the most terrifying aspect of relationships everyone told me was amazing and hot and felt unimaginably good. Intimacy. Sex. The unearthing of desire I was too afraid to reveal until he came into my life.

For me, sex was riddled with pain, abuse, chaos, and shame. It's how I came to know about sex from my two mothers: the whore and the virgin. One mother made me fear sex because of her occupation as a prostitute and the second one taught me the shame that comes with it when she called me a whore, just like my birth mother, whenever I disobeyed her.

I was stuck in the middle — a virgin who believed that true love with one man would ease me into the rite of passage everyone expected me to embrace in my twenties without fear or shame. But I was an aberration. Boys feared me, and girls felt threatened by me. My virginity made girls feel like sluts while their boyfriends feared their girls would hold out on the thing that made them feel connected. I was derided and mocked for my virginity. There was something wrong with me.

But I didn't feel that way in my twenties. I felt strong, impervious to passion and the phoniness that comes with believing sex is always about love. I was in control, not only of my body and its desires but also of the boys who wanted it, who would use it and then run from it.

Use me. And then run from me once they got what they wanted. No one would use me. Not for sex. Not on my watch.

In my childhood, sex was not about love. It was about power and manipulation. It was transactional, with a price I wasn't willing to pay just for a few minutes of pleasure. Every time a guy dumped me because I wouldn't give in to his sexual needs was proof to me that boys expect sex for simple things like taking you out on a date or buying you a drink or the cost of a movie with soda and popcorn. You want Raisinets, too? What will you give him for them?

Or maybe there *was* something wrong with me. But with two mothers who defined sex for me, polarized it for me, remaining a virgin until I was ready to rid myself of the purity *V* was key to my survival. Key to my self-respect. The only key I had to loving myself the way my mothers had not. To force boys to love me the way men had not loved my first mother. On my terms. I had to fend for myself. Nurture my own needs. Protect my body.

When Richard came into my life, sex was not the basis of our relationship. Sure, we fooled around. I experienced many of my firsts with him, but as much as I loved him, I needed to know he also loved me, the girl beneath the skin and bones and curves comprising my outer shell. And this he did in unique and personal ways that mattered to someone like me who only knew familial rejection and denial.

He drove me wherever I needed to go and picked me up from my night classes to make sure I didn't have to wait at the bus stop, in the middle of winter, to get home from my college campus in Flushing. He bought me heated gloves for the nights and days he couldn't get to me. He even bought me a winter coat, since I waded through winter in jeans and sweaters, daring the winds and storms of the season to overtake me with the flu. He met me on my way to work with a bagel and coffee.

And he fed me. He cooked for me in his small kitchen, chicken dinners to make up for the fact I had only eaten a donut that day or french fries from Roy Rogers, which I picked on during the day between work and school because it was all I could afford.

He was the first boy to see me naked, to lie down next to me on his bed, and touch all the parts of me that remained hidden from male eyes and hands. I learned about oral sex with him, and it was always reciprocal, earth-shatteringly rare for me who never orgasmed or masturbated until he came into my life in my midtwenties to show me how.

He was my teacher in all things. He taught me how to drive, how to cook, and how to enjoy sex without penetration. I didn't feel dirty after a night out with Richard, and the memory of his hands on my skin, my breasts, his fingers inside me didn't incite a thorough scrubbing of my flesh afterward. I wanted his touch on me, the smell of him stuck to the sweat between my thighs. I was in love, and sex was the next natural step.

So why don't I remember the first time we had sex?

I worked so hard to maintain my purity until it felt right to give it up, to give in to adulthood and adult matters, and then not to recall the first time—it's a strange occurrence. Especially because I remember everything. I hold onto memories with the dysfunction of a hoarder who cannot let anything go. I collect memories with compulsion, prying each one apart for lost treasure. But for the life of me, I don't remember the first time. I remember all the times we fooled around before and some of the sex we had during our marriage. There wasn't that much.

What I do remember are all the times Richard and I tried,

and the pain and discomfort that came with each attempt. We often attempted to go all the way, but the pain was intolerable for me. My thighs clenched the way my jaw clenches now when I am stressed or anticipating a bad omen in my life, my teeth gnashing against each other in my sleep, forcing me to wake with raw and bleeding gums. I sealed my eyes shut and held onto his arms, waiting for the pain to wash over me. I even tried alcohol, drinking wine or beer to make my limbs numb enough to slip into a missionary position and have the entire ordeal be over. But nothing worked.

I recently watched *Unorthodox*, a movie based on a true story about a young Hasidic Jewish girl married off to a man in the community and the agony she endured with her first time having sex. She was young, eighteen, and a virgin, of course. For months after her wedding, she couldn't go through with sex. Her body tightened, the pain was excruciating, and the anticipation made it even worse. Of course, she didn't love her husband. This was an arranged marriage, and there was no foreplay or arousal involved.

It took months, the involvement of the community, and finally, the threat of divorce to force her to have sex. With tears in her eyes, she told him to keep going, past the pain, past the discomfort, to break the virgin wall until he exploded inside of her with effortless zeal.

Afterward, she clung to the sheet covering her nakedness, sobbing, and he exclaimed something like, "That was amazing," oblivious to her own torment.

I loved Richard, and our foreplay lasted for hours, but when it came down to actual penetration, my story collided with this girl's own version. I was forty-eight when I watched this film, based on the girl's memoir, and this was the first time I could say I was not alone. It was the first time I came across anyone describing my own experiences with sex.

Women I know tell me their first time was not memorable, or

it was a hurried experience they participated in just to lose their virginity. Very few tell me it was wonderful. No one has ever echoed my own experiences with the pain, the fear, the exhaustion of forcing my body to go through the trials of sexual coupling while stiff as a rock with trepidation.

It's interesting, looking back now, at how my sexual dysfunction, if that's what it is, somehow aligned with Richard's. When I was in my twenties, loving him, being loved by him, I thought he was waiting for me, patiently loving the fears out of me one by one until I was ready for the love he offered—a love that no other boy had been willing to show me, or wait around long enough to give me without expecting me to reciprocate with my sex.

I thought he was different. And perhaps he was all those things, but he also lacked confidence when it came to sex, especially when his partners were sexually aggressive. His insecurities made him a perfect match for me when it came to sex. I was a virgin, and in our coupling, he was my teacher. We were two sexual puzzles and somehow, in the huge, dilapidated, and congested boroughs of New York, Richard and I fell into each other's dysfunctions with blind faith and called it fate.

Once we were married, the facade slipped off our shoulders like water sliding down hot skin. Smooth and with slow, tedious degrees. We didn't have sex on our wedding night. We were too tired and agreed it wasn't written anywhere in the books of love and marriage that we had to have sex. We sprawled our wedding cards on the floor, counted the money we received from our friends and family, and packed for our trip to Hawaii the following morning.

Even during our honeymoon, there was this pressure to have sex, but we only did it once. It was forced, something we felt we had to do, get out of the way, like a burden weighing on our shoulders, bending our spines out of alignment. And then Richard got a sunburn because he refused to put sun protection on his pink, Irish skin. It was the kind of burn that made him walk and talk like an automaton, agitated by any slight movement that made his skin stretch against itself. I couldn't touch him. He couldn't even smile. Sex was out of the question. Neither one of us wanted it.

And I remember being relieved. There was no expectation to have sex, to don the lingerie gifted to me during my bridal shower, pretending I was a normal sexual being who enjoyed dressing up in feminine attire designed to turn him on so he could ravage me. That shit remained at the bottom of my suitcase for the seven days and six nights we spent in Kauai, Richard nursing his sunburn with alcohol while I was made love to by the sun's intense rays, his fingers trailing over my skin as I bathed in his light, goosebumps erect and arching to meet his touch.

We were reluctant lovers even before our kids were born. Sex was the thing we did because there was some societal voice injecting itself into our marital home and bed telling us there was a gnawing dysfunction in our midst unless we had intercourse at least once a week. We bought a sex game and alcohol, mixing the two on a Saturday night so we could couple the way proper couples did. With our genitals, naked, sweaty, and sticky. Afterward, we were always relieved that we'd had sex, that we made it all the way to climax without shrinkage or impatience or burning aches in places that couldn't be seen or touched.

"God," he would say to me, lying on his back, breathing in heavy bursts. "I forgot how good this feels."

"Yeah," I would huff and puff back, wondering how long I should wait before running to the bathroom to clean myself out and dab a cold, wet cloth between my legs to ease the pain that coursed through my insides without insulting him. "We should do this more often."

I wasn't lying. Back then.

The only aspects of sex I enjoyed were the foreplay, the orgasms, and the way I felt connected to Richard. He was the love of my life, and as long as we had sex, we would remain connected. But when it came to actual pleasure, the thing I anticipated and longed for revolved around touch. All the time. Hugs were pleasurable. A kiss on the nape of my neck. His fingers coiled around my brown, knotted hair. The simple interlacing of our fingers as we sat side-by-side at the movie theater or in the car or on our living room couch.

That was natural for me. That was love. Not sex. Sex was always an afterthought. A chore. Something worthy of procrastination, like a research paper without a deadline, or not mowing the lawn until HOA left a letter in our mailbox with a deadline to get it done. Or else.

Though I don't remember the first time Richard went all the way through me, into me, I remember more the burning pain after sex. It took days for the rawness to fade, and I never orgasmed during sex unless it included clitoral stimulation. There was always that gnawing feeling in my bones that made me feel dirty for having sex, a voice inside my head laughing at me, calling me a *putana* for being wanton, desirous.

Sex was never easy for me. There was something about it that left me unsituated in my own body, like it didn't belong to me, or at least, I didn't want it to. Maybe it was because pleasure was the sticky thing I was denying myself. Maybe it was because my earliest memories of sex came to me wrapped in a cloak of shame and my birth mother's prostitution, something men took when they wanted and paid for.

"Why would you want to deny yourself the simple pleasures of sex?" my female friends asked me when I told them I hadn't had sex in over a decade.

"There's nothing simple about sex," I told them. Sex complicates everything. The way you see yourself, the way you see your partner, the way we let critical issues slip away from us—because sex gets in the way. Because sex and pleasure cloud problems settling into you like a bag full of rocks, drowning the complexities that return after the orgasms. Like lack of communication. Like being called a bitch and a cunt during a heated fight. Like being told he feels nothing for you anymore except anger.

"It hurts when I have sex," I told my gynecologist back then.

"You're probably tense. Have some wine. Use some lube. It'll get easier," was her advice. But I wanted more from her. I wanted her to seek the answers deep inside my vaginal canal, to explore the history of its making and assure me everything was all right. She didn't. She only tested for cysts or yeast infections or the annual pap smear and hardly looked into my eyes.

She was all business. In and out of my vagina. In and out of the office with a distracted smile on her pale face.

Why can't I enjoy sex? I wanted to scream at her. But I didn't. I was not comfortable enough to yell at her, to demand she help me figure out what was wrong with me.

I bought lingerie instead. And lube. The lube helped, but the lingerie made me uncomfortable. Richard liked it, the silky fabric falling smoothly and easily off my shoulders, clinging to the tips of my nipples before he replaced it with his mouth. It was sexy for him. I closed my eyes and tried to enjoy the sensations, only to tense up again when it was time for penetration. I gritted my teeth while his voice told me to relax, a raspy whisper in my ears.

I tried to like lingerie, but it was like wearing dresses and skirts and putting on makeup and heels. They were intended to feminize me, make me small and slutty and soft for the taking. Make me desirable. And I felt desirable, but I also felt like a whore. Even though I was already in love and married, I was dressing up for my husband, for his arousal, so he could continue to crave me.

Why do women have to wear lingerie to be desired by their men? By any man? It's a reduction to the sole purpose of my being as a sexual object, desirous in its femininity, a fantasy that turns men on. And what should turn *me* on? The lingerie? No.

Lingerie is for men, not women. Richard's desire for me is supposed to turn me on. Turning him on is supposed to turn me on. Him first. Me second. I can't live this kind of life. I don't believe my role is to please him, to want to please him, sexually or otherwise. There's more to me than my sex.

I have watched shows on top of shows, written and directed by men, in which beautiful women married to ugly, fat comedians objectify themselves to be loved so they don't lose the affections of their men.

One woman dresses like a hot maid on Halloween night with the promise of role play after the kids have gone to bed—while he's dressed in jeans and a sweatshirt.

Another one puts a stripper pole in the bedroom and begins taking pole dancing lessons, so she can dance and strip for him before sex. He sits on the bed, fat and fully dressed, watching her, his fingers itching to slip a twenty-dollar bill into her panties.

In yet another, the husband gets physical with his fictional wife, pushing her on the bed, on her stomach, shoves her head down on the mattress, and takes her from behind. A mock rape. And the writers of the show decided that she would like this— him taking what he wants with force, without foreplay, without caring if she orgasmed or not. It was about domination, and she wanted her own husband to physically overcome her.

Rape her.

That's a man's fantasy. A man who doesn't understand the difference between erotic sex and rape. A man who has never known rape. Rape is never a woman's fantasy. It's her darkest fear.

When passion fades, women are being taught to turn themselves inside out—play-acting as hookers, strippers, pole dancers, slutty nurses, and ditsy cheerleaders to remind men of their sexual appeal. And we buy into it because we are being told, repeatedly, that we are nothing without the love of our men—and by love, I mean the sexual love, the sexual desire.

Because love is a whole other animal. It's the thing keeping you together without sex. It's what remains when sex is no longer on the table. It's the sweet spot of a relationship that exists when a man wants to be with you because of you, not because he wants to get into your sex at any cost to your identity and self-respect.

I don't like dressing up for sex, being desired because of a fantasy, an unreal and unrealistic depiction of who I am. I don't like pretending to be a hot, slutty, sexy stripper so my husband will want to have sex with me. I don't like playing pretend games. I am not an object, and I don't like to be treated like one, especially by my husband, in my marriage, where I should be reminded each day that I am loved for me. That the woman in me is loved—not the sex in me.

After all, I loved him for him, despite his tempers and his immaturity. He didn't need to pretend to be someone else for me to want him—someone hotter or sexier. He didn't need to wear lingerie for me to desire him.

Why should I?

WEINSTEIN AND LOOKING
THE OTHER WAY

The day Richard and I married, on a balmy July evening that threatened to rain, almost forcing us away from the gazebo nuptials I wanted, I told myself to look the other way whenever something awkward or irritating occurred.

When my mother harassed our photographer, telling him how to angle the light, that she had been in the photography business, and that his hold on the camera was incorrect, I smiled and looked the other way.

When my mother's cousin Angie reprimanded me during the reception because I spent most of my time on the dance floor with my friends and didn't spend my wedding day strolling from table to table like a gracious bride was supposed to, I smiled and looked the other way.

Even when Richard ignored my insistence that Ann was not to be included in the reception party since she refused to walk me down the aisle when I asked her to give me away, and he made her part of our wedding party, I looked the other way then, too.

When she told me I was the silliest bride she had ever encountered, because I was bouncing on my toes during the vows, half-giggling and half-crying, I averted my gaze from her mocking one. I smiled. I was polite. I looked the other way.

I don't know where I picked up this trick, this morsel of

advice that must have been given to me at some point, but I followed it with strict adherence, and no gray clouds broke through the surface of my wedding day. Nothing bothered me that day. And at some point, this concept of looking the other way became very natural to me, very seductive, so that I applied it to all other areas of my life, in my marriage, and most especially in my dealings with both my mother and Richard.

I smiled and looked the other way when Richard's friends came to our apartment and started scrolling through my new computer for porn, one that I bought for my first teaching job in New York. This was a hard pill for me to swallow because they all knew I was a feminist, that I saw pornography as objectifying women forced into the sex industry either for survival or because of trauma.

I never looked away from my feminism. Never tucked her in a corner or under the bed to please anyone. In fact, speaking about my feminist ideologies gave me the voice I lacked in all other areas of my life. It was the only thing I was confident about, sure about, felt solid about. In my feminist clothes, I was never weak or weakened. I was a warrior.

But in my new role as wife, I began looking the other way, smiling while gently addressing the fact that my computer was not intended for pornography. There was a part of me that expected Richard to stop them, to turn off my computer, not to laugh along with his friends as they moved from image to image of female vaginas. And in front of me. As if I were one of them. One of the boys. I wanted to see how Richard would react, how he would handle that kind of peer pressure, and it surprised me when he didn't reject porn or tell the guys they were disrespecting me.

I smiled and looked away when, one after the other, his friends got engaged and prepared for their bachelor parties. His friends were each born into culturally patriarchal backgrounds situated in drinking and frequenting strip clubs while flicking from one porn site to the next.

This was a norm for them. Natural. What a man did for fun, for release, even if it meant he did it behind his girlfriend's back, or in the middle of the night, while she slept in another room.

Bachelor parties meant one thing: strippers. Nothing I could condone or feel good about when Richard went to one after the other until they were all married and graduated to strip clubs as married men. Each time, I got upset, had a long conversation with Richard, and each time, he went, refusing to sit out a strip club or a celebration of each guy's last night as a free man. I never asked what happened or how Richard participated. I heard from the other wives or girlfriends that there were strippers, whipped cream licked off nipples, and body shots. None of it left me feeling proud or happy. It was not something I liked about Richard, even though I loved him.

"There's nothing wrong with strippers," he scoffed at me. "This is all you. Your hang-ups about sex."

Yes, I had hang-ups. My mother was a prostitute, and I left that part of my childhood in the past, where it belonged. But I was also a feminist, not the kind of feminist who believed in sex work as liberatory, because the sex work in my childhood was not liberatory or empowering for the women involved. It was abusive, aggressive, a celebration of masculinity and male prowess that left the women they used as expendable objects, easily re-placed, easily abandoned, easily paid for.

He knew my history. He understood my views. He dismissed me anyway. And I learned to look the other way because we were married, we were in love, and there was nothing I could say to make him listen to me. Respect me. Do the opposite of what his friends expected him to do as a man.

I looked the other way, years later, when I dropped off Joseph and Rena at his job so I could go to my part-time teaching position as a community college adjunct in North Carolina. By this time, he had left his boys behind in New York, but he worked in an all-male industry with an all-male crew. And as I pushed Rena's stroller into his office and released Joseph's hand from my grasp to remove her from the belted seat, I caught a glimpse of the screensaver on his computer.

It was a picture of a beautiful brunette, scantily clad, with big breasts and a thong bikini, her lips puckered and ready for a blow job—presumably. He immediately turned it off, not so much because I'd seen it and looked at him with disgust, but because our four-year-old son had seen it as well.

"That was just a joke," he said, laughing nervously. "Hey buddy!" He took the time to grab Joseph and pull him onto his lap as he continued to trade the company's money. "The guys around here, they like to joke around by sending these pics," he insisted, his eyes shifting to the rate changes of the stocks he was following on the screen.

"That was a screensaver," I pointed out to him. I wasn't stupid. But I turned away then, too, and left my kids to go to work. I didn't smile then. I was taken aback. Where was the guy I had met ten years earlier, who had chosen me because I was cool and sober and cute and sexy without being provocative? Who was this guy who shared photos of nearly naked girls with other men he worked with?

Once, I even caught him comparing images of hot girls with his friend Neil when his text messages somehow started pinging on my computer. I deleted his account so I couldn't see any more. By this point, I was tired of the fights, the disagreements about his never being able to suspend his appetite to please his friends. Perhaps even his own desire to objectify women while he was raising a little girl and married to a feminist—one he had chosen because of her strength, her views, even her feminism.

Looking the other way became a habit. A way to ignore the

fact that the man I loved was like every other man who deemed girls as sexual prey—even though he knew my history with sex, my triggers with sexual depravity. Even though he knew how important female empowerment was to me. Female empowerment that had nothing to do with women using their bodies and sex to acquire equal status in a patriarchal society.

I looked the other way to keep the peace. To stop the panic spreading in my chest like wildfire, leaving behind carnage and smoke that remained unresolved and irreparable. I looked the other way out of fear of rages that came at me like sharpened daggers, reopening old wounds Richard helped me place Band-Aids over—once.

A long time ago.

Before kids. Before marriage. Before disdain and contempt eroded into our marriage and the love I perceived as real and deep. The balm that had once cleared away the bruises of my childhood began to fade. I looked the other way until there were no smiles left. No laughter. No desire to continue the facade that had become our marriage.

I turned looking the other way into an art until ignoring everything he said and did no longer served a purpose. Until I knew we wouldn't last and when love no longer lingered between us. Had abandoned our home and hearts with no trace of return.

Without love in me, without laughter or lightness, I could no longer look the other way. I planted my feet and faced the derision, the consequences that came with no longer avoiding the reality of our existence as parents, husband and wife, Marina and Richard.

Like most men, Richard liked to grab my butt or cup my breasts outside of the bedroom. In the kitchen. In the living room. Out on the back porch.

"Stop grabbing me," I told him repeatedly.

"Why? You're my wife."

"It doesn't make me your possession. I don't go around grabbing your ass or your balls, do I?"

"I'd love it if you did." He kissed me on the cheek to show me his earnestness. "Anyway, those are my breasts, my ass," he continued, cupping my breasts for demonstration.

"No," I told him, pulling away from him. "This is my body, my breasts, my ass. They don't belong to you because we are married."

But he never quite understood this. It is the normative assumption among men that in marriage, women belong to them — including their sexualized parts. My friend, Shirley, once asked if Richard grabbed my breasts whenever he stepped on the brake while driving.

"You, too?" I asked. We laughed then, years ago, in our late twenties. They were immature guys, but we loved them. It's how they showed their affection, their desire for us, we told ourselves.

But for someone like me who needs boundaries when it comes to touch and sex, it was an irritating argument to have recycled during the twenty-two years of our marriage.

Richard also did this while we weren't having sex, when we had just begun not having sex but living and parenting together, pecks passed from lips to lips and inevitably from lips to cheeks. When he continued to smack my butt or grab a breast during our celibate years, my body reacted with revulsion, stiffening, my jaw clenched in anger.

"Stop grabbing me."

"You're my wife."

"I don't consent to you touching me like that. We're not intimate. We haven't been intimate in ten years. So quit it."

He sulked and moved away from me. Then returned for the last word.

"What kind of message do you think we're sending our kids?" he asked, visibly angry with me. "They're learning from us about intimacy in relationships."

I stopped washing the dishes and turned to him. "I'm not going to pretend to be intimate with you so our kids can have a false image of what marriage is. I'm not doing that."

He walked away. He was reading a self-help book about staying in his seat of consciousness and not reacting with anger. It worked sometimes but not always. I saw how hard he was trying to master his emotions, not blowing up at me because I had stopped talking to him about my feelings, stopped having sex with him, stopped reaching out to him for hugs and kisses.

When the #metoo movement went viral, and sexual allegation charges against Weinstein were all over the media, the image of a fat, ugly, piggish-looking man with a hairy chest, his penis lolling about as he chased beautiful women around the suite of his hotel for a blow job made me sick to my stomach. It reminded me of how men feel entitled to women because they are men, because they have needs, because they have some kind of power over them. He reminded me of my teachers — the males I encountered in my childhood, at work, and on dates — sex always at the center of their attention, regardless of the woman who should have ownership and rights over her body and sex.

The next time Richard grabbed my butt in the kitchen, trying to show our kids we were loving and intimate and "normal," I readied myself for a fight.

"Stop manhandling me, Weinstein," I threw the insult at him. He stopped and looked at me, the smile gone from his face.

"Weinstein?"

"Yeah. Weinstein. I've told you I don't want you grabbing me, but you still do it. That's Weinstein's way."

He gave me a scathing look and walked away. Back in his seat of consciousness.

He continued to grab me, my breasts, I suppose out of habit. But each time, I called him Weinstein, reminding him that even in marriage, women get to have a say as to who can and cannot touch them. And when. And how. Eventually he stopped, and for the first time in our ten full years of non-intimate marriage, I felt comfortable walking around my house knowing no hands would reach out for me and grab me in the way I didn't want to be grabbed. Even if those hands belonged to the man I had once given my heart and love to, my body did not belong to him. It never should.

There was a time, a long time ago, when I was overwhelmed by this aching need to touch him. My hands itched to trace the rippling vein meandering from his finely shaped scalp to the tip of his earlobe, to feel the throbbing pulse of his heartbeat on my fingertips, especially when he was sitting beside me, on the opposite corner of the couch, unaware I was looking at him, taking slow sips of him as if he were my favorite port wine. My eyes digested the slight bulge of the potbelly he could no longer hide beneath his T-shirts, the short golden hair covering his knobby knees, the legs stretching out until they found a resting place along the edges of our living room table, the cherry-colored veneer of its surface looking as aged and cracked and scratched as our twenty-two-year marriage. But that was a long time ago.

His body was a body I used to know well, but one I began to avoid at all costs, shrinking to a smaller size when his arms enclosed me in an embrace that left me gasping for open space. He brushed his hips against my backside when we reached for the same bowl or drinking glass in the kitchen cabinets, and I quickly moved away from him, as if his skin were on fire, evading the touch of his hands, hands that used to love me tenderly. It all seems so long ago.

His body eventually became just a body. A stranger's limbs, unknown to mine. His nearness made my body, small and furtive, disappear into itself, hiding from him like a child folding herself to fit into tight corners. I covered my nakedness when he walked in on me undressing in the closet, avoiding his eyes, unsure if they consumed a breast or a thigh against my will. I turned my back to him as he fished for keys and business cards.

"See ya later," he mumbled.

"See ya," I responded, my back still to him, holding my breath until I heard his feet disappear down the stairs and out the front door.

There was a time he would have kissed me.

There was a time I would have turned for that kiss, closed my eyes, and puckered in anticipation, my breasts, post-child-birth flabby belly, and naked hips arching and opening toward him with a hunger only his lips and hands could feed. But no more.

My body is mine. And his body is his. And for a while, the two existed in separate spheres of lonely space surrounding us, passing each other in hallways and kitchens and children's bedrooms as we took turns kissing them good night, sweet dreams, don't let the bed bugs bite.

There were times, early on during my forced abstinence, when I ached to touch him. Just one caress along his freckled arm, the nape of his neck, a soft kiss on his cheek. It only took one touch, a small gesture, and all of it—the debris of our un-finished fights, the uncommunicative angst, the hurt we dished out like leftover dinners—would dissipate into small crumbs gathered and scraped into the trash can for good. But my arms remained heavy on my lap like stubborn, rooted rocks, grinding against my legs, pushing me further into my corner and the si-lence I have learned to rely on as my asylum.

For a while, before I left our marriage, I wanted to touch him most when he looked at me, his head turning slightly toward me, when his green eyes took hold of mine, twinkling with humor. He wouldn't touch me then. He knew I would pull away, and my references to Weinstein crippled him from pursuing me.

But he let his eyes touch me. And they felt warm on me,

washing away the coldness with which I covered my skin. I smiled back, wishing we could love each other only with our eyes, speak to one another through them, without the words we glazed with arsenic and resentment.

Eyes are guileless. Love still lives in them, and it haunts us with memories of what we were like when our eyes first met, kissed, loved. Before words got in the way and twisted us beyond recognition.

There was a time I ached to break the yawning space we negotiated around each other without words or love or touch.

But then he spoke. Or yelled. Or raged.

And ice ran through me like a storm, cooling my body until it stood there, in front of him, rigid and hollow.

Untouchable.

Impenetrable.

And unsexed.

SUICIDEATIONS

"*I* want a divorce."

These words came out of Richard's mouth about twelve years ago. I had just taught an evening class at Wake Tech and was sitting on the brown leather couch in our bonus room, eating mozzarella balls with my fingers and watching *Law and Order: Criminal Intent*.

His words came out of nowhere.

He came into the room quietly and stood against the wall to my left. My eyes were still riveted to the flashing lights on the screen, not really paying attention to the dialogue or action of the show since I had watched it from beginning to end at least three times already. It was just something to watch. To keep my brain busy. To keep my fears silent and placid, asleep inside of me until the next day began, and they awakened along with my children, their laughter or cries or whines inviting them to come out and play.

I held my breath but didn't say anything. I couldn't even look at him. I was stunned.

He continued.

"I don't feel anything for you anymore." There was a yawning pause. I held my breath. "Just anger," he added as an afterthought.

I kept my eyes glued to the television set so as not to make the moment real, something I needed to face. A talk I didn't want or expect to have. I could feel him watching me, for some kind of response, but after a few long minutes of silence, he walked away as quietly as he had arrived, his footsteps light as they drifted down the back stairs.

I exhaled. My breaths came out in shudders, the way they did when my teeth chattered while waiting for buses during the winter nights in New York. The air was too cold, too icy to take into my body—a body that went rigid without warmth, resembling a pale ghost no one saw long enough to care about. My lungs constricted, as if someone squeezed their center, deriding me while I struggled for oxygen, for one long, tremulous breath of wanting air.

I sat in the same spot for a few more hours until I heard him go to bed, waited another hour, and then crawled into bed beside him. My body turned into itself, facing the opposite direction, my heart clanging against my chest with fear he would say more to me. He didn't.

The next day, I drove to work in a daze. It took me a few minutes of red-and-blue lights flashing behind me to realize I was being pulled over for speeding. In all the years I had been driving, I had never been stopped by the cops.

"It's my first time getting pulled over," I told the police officer, hearing the erratic vibrations in my voice, my hands shaking with trepidation on the steering wheel. Partly because he was an authority figure, and partly because I was on the verge of tears, ready to tell him the truth. That the man I put all my hopes and fears and dreams into no longer loved me. What was I to do now? I only had a part-time job. I had been out of work for years while raising the little ones. How was I supposed to live? To care for myself? To care for them without a stable job in place?

I found myself in every dire situation I promised myself I would never get into: I had given up my job to care for my children until the man I loved no longer loved me and wanted to push me out of the family I'd made from nothing. From ashes.

From childhood dysfunction and parental neglect Richard and I had vowed not to replicate.

But I kept it all in, all together. The officer let me go with a warning while everything I feared about the trajectory of my life became a reality I had encountered only in other couples, in books, and in *Lifetime* movies.

I still recall the helplessness I felt that night, sitting in the bonus room and digesting the words he had uttered in the dark room of our home. How mute his confession made me, how lost I felt in my own thoughts. He didn't love me. What had I done to lose the love he had inscribed on my wedding band as "unconditional"?

For two nights, I sank into depths that came to me only in my direst times. When I felt I had no control over my life. I began to make plans, drawing out different paths to pursue my desire without hurting everyone in the process. When I had one in place, I sat on the back porch and typed a letter addressed to Richard on my laptop. I saved it as "My last will and testament," so he would find it if he went looking for it in my files.

"It's not your fault," I wrote to him. "Don't blame yourself for my choices. This is something I've wanted to do for a long time. Tell Joseph and Rena I love them."

On the third morning after his confession, I drove the kids to school and returned home. I grabbed Richard's oxycodone pills, the ones he used for his back pains, and planned out the closing chapter of my life. I intended to drive to the back of the Barnes & Noble parking lot, because it was usually empty of cars and people, and swallow all the pills in the container.

My only problem was that I didn't want to return or be brought back, like Sylvia Plath, during her first two attempts at suicide. I wanted my death to be immediate and decisive. Forever. I wanted to do it right this time.

Before moving forward with the plan, I googled how many pills to take based on my weight. I had heard of people attempting to kill themselves with the wrong number of pills in their system, which only meant they were forced back to life against their will. Like Plath. I didn't want that.

But what I found on the internet was not an exact ratio of pills to my weight to give me the relief I sought. What I found instead were faceless phrases and pleas that forced my eyes to widen and my hand to cover the camera on my computer, fearful someone on the other side of the screen saw me.

I had been found out.

"Don't do it," one person wrote. "I tried it and here I am, completely dependent on my loved ones to take care of me."

"Think of the ones you leave behind," another said. "Think of your family, the ones who love you."

"Nothing is ever this bad. Seek the help you need to stay here. Here's my cell. Call me. We can talk."

"You are loved. There will be an emptiness if you go," wrote another one.

"Don't do it," a collective string of voices reached out to me, their hands grabbing my wrists and ankles to keep me there, in front of the computer, where they could see me. And to keep me there, in the life I so wanted to end.

I inadvertently clicked on a site intended to stop suicides. I'd been tricked. I found myself seen and cared for by a slew of strangers writing about people they had lost to suicide, logging onto this site to save someone in return. People who'd attempted suicide were writing about their failed experiences, finding God or love, and reasons to stay in a life they once wanted to leave, too. Just like me.

I pushed my chair away from the computer and checked my camera to make sure they couldn't see me. I noticed the dates on the messages. They had been written months and years earlier. No one knew me, but here they were, trying to save me. They saw me without seeing me. They caught me as I fell into the pit of self-loathing, rocks stuffed in my pockets, pressing me down until I no longer had to force myself to breathe.

They said they loved me even if I didn't love myself enough to want to live. I was a ghost, caressed by tender voices and words meant for any number of us who found ourselves on this site while trying to research the best way to kill ourselves.

I turned off the computer and slumped onto the floor like a heap of melted skin without bones to hold it up. I curled into a ball, grabbing the attention of Morpheus, our Golden Retriever, his wet nose trying to sniff out the problem. I lay there, away from the computer and its screen, just in case there was someone out there who could see me. Bring me back with love. With kindness.

I began to sob.

Not from relief.

From grief. This was the third time in my life I had wanted to die, imagined, and planned out my death only to be denied the absence I so craved. Because of cowardice. Because of guilt.

My cowardice. My guilt.

The first time occurred during the summer between my twelfth and thirteenth birthday. I locked myself in the bathroom and attempted to ram a pair of scissors into my chest, praying for the relief I knew would come with a hole in my skin to match the holes inside me, blood spilling out of the shell that held me together. I figured if my birth family and my adoptive mother didn't love me, no one else would.

I certainly held no love for myself. I thought that if I took myself out of the equation, then we would all be happy. My birth family wouldn't have to bear the weight of abandoning me and my adoptive mother would be free to adopt a nice, smart Asian girl who would play the violin without having a baking timer set for fifteen minutes each day. In fact, this ideal daughter would play for an hour. Even two.

By the time I was twelve, Ann had ripped my roots from my

body, and it only lolled and rolled like a formless thing without a spine to hold it up, not belonging or attaching properly to anything grounded or secure. It just was. Empty. A void. What was the harm in hurting myself, in making me disappear if I couldn't be seen, anyway?

I tried to jam a hole in me wide enough that the rest of me could easily pour out and spill onto my sneakers, but each time the scissors made contact with my chest, they froze. It reminded me of the dreams I'd had, violent dreams where I was straddling a faceless man and throwing punches at his face. But each time my knuckles touched his cheek, my fists bounced off, like there was some kind of rubber surface between us. I couldn't strike him, no matter how forceful the attack was when it began. My punches bounced off, too, leaving increased rage burning inside my chest, my fists aching with the desire to destroy and drive his face into the center of his skull.

This is how stabbing myself felt, even though I was no longer in a dream state. Sitting on the toilet seat, I could see my face in the mirror opposite me, the crooked bangs concealing the top of my bloodshot eyes, brown masks I taught myself to wear that hid names and stories and feelings behind its muddy depths. Thin lips lay like a flattened line against my face, opening only slightly to breathe in the courage needed to try again.

And I did try again. But the scissor tips stopped at my shirt again and punctured a small hole into the cotton fabric. The rage and need to hurt myself vibrated into an imperceptible hum, leaving me hunched and helpless, the scissors dangling from trembling fingertips, brittle nails bitten down to the stumped nail beds, puffy with angry red lesions and hangnails my teeth couldn't pry from my skin.

I gave up then and returned to bed, feeling my way in the dark, my mother never knowing my intentions. I've never told her. My tongue is too tangled inside my mouth, and words feel like marbles sliding to the back of my throat whenever I consider opening my mouth to say, "I hurt. You hurt me."

I remain silent. Even now. Only my body speaks of its pain, the way it goes cold and tense, reverting to rigid lines of bones and muscles that have atrophied from lack of touch. From absent love.

The second time suicide became an option for me, I was the thirty-five-year-old mother of a small, toddling boy, Joseph, unable to handle the requirements of motherhood. I spent my entire day with him from early morning feedings to five or six in the evening when Richard came home from work.

Sometimes, he didn't come home until eleven at night. I called him to find out that he was three or four hours away. He'd had a grueling day at work and wanted to drive it off and not bring anger and frustration home. Or he had gone out with his friends for drinks, staggering into our bedroom hours past midnight, reeking of beer and smoke.

The day I accidentally locked Joseph in the car, I couldn't get in touch with Richard. He had turned off his phone, and I wept as the firemen forced my car open to pull my screaming son out. He and I were stranded at the Walt Whitman Mall for hours afterward, and when I called Richard's job, they told me he was out. My keys were still locked inside my car. With all the chaos, it did not occur to me to get my keys out through the trunk of the car while the firemen rescued my son. I called Richard's brother-in-law to pick me up.

Without my keys, I couldn't get into the house, so Joseph and I stayed with my in-laws until I located Richard. I had to call Lexus and ask them to alert my husband through the SOS link in his car while he was driving. He was three hours away, and it wasn't until midnight that I laid Joseph down in his own crib, in our own house.

On the days his car rolled into our driveway right after work, I was out the door and into my car, unable to get out of there fast

enough. I often went to the movies on my own, escaping my role
as wife and mother for a few brief hours. Or I went to the mall
and treated myself to Starbucks.

Or I drove on the highway, veered onto the left lane, and
stepped on the gas, going as fast as my cowardice would allow,
shutting my eyes and holding my breath, all in the hopes my car
would hit the divider, lose control, and flip me over, casting me
into the darkness I yearned for.

I imagined death a lot in those days because that was the
most I ever felt like a failure—a failing mom, a failed human being—and all I wanted was to feel nothing, to be taken out of my
situation by force with no hope for return. Darkness and quiet
and stillness were what I desired more than being loved and
needed by my husband and child. Maybe a nanny would have
helped. Or a preschool to give me the few hours each day I needed
to myself, to be myself, to at least figure out who I really was,
outside of Richard and our son. Outside of the skins of motherhood and wife that didn't seem to fit me all too well.

I had no one to talk to in those days, and when I voiced my
frustrations with playing the stay-at-home mom and how unsuited
I was for it, Richard's hazel eyes filled with the disappointment I
had often found in my adoptive mother's eyes—after she adopted
me and realized I was not worthy of her affections.

"I sacrifice for our family by going to work," he told me.
"You sacrifice by staying home and taking care of Joseph. Only
until he's old enough."

But I hadn't quit my job to take care of our son a few years
earlier. I had quit my teaching job to write. To be a writer. And to
get my PhD in English, attending classes twice a week in the
evenings.

When I pointed this out to him, he nodded. "Exactly. Take
care of Joseph during the day and you when I get home. Go to
school, do your assignments, and write on the weekends."

It all seemed so easy when he put it out there like that. But it was harder for me. And more so because my frustrations as a new and inexperienced mother had nowhere to go but my son, so I often went out to my backyard and screamed them aloud into the wind, wishing someone would hear me and come to my aid.

But no one did, not even my hero. My husband. The man I once called my best friend. I was all alone, with only Richard's disappointment following me about the house, looking over my shoulder to ensure I fed our son correctly, put him down to nap at the right time, took him out for daily strolls, exposed him to museums and other children at the park.

"Did you take him out today?" Richard asked when he got home. If my answer was no, he would shake his head. "He needs to get out. You have to socialize him."

But taking him out caused me anxiety. I was grown. But I was scared, too. Petrified of being alone with my son, his little smiling face and fragile body and mind dependent on me. For someone like me, who had no experience with children—never babysat, never really wanted to—being responsible for a toddler overwhelmed me. What if I failed? I'd already locked him in my car and watched him sink in the pool, unable to stop him from falling on his face and chipping his tooth. I was too inexperienced, too uneasy with the responsibility of his life in my hands—my most incompetent hands that trembled whenever he fell and skinned a knee.

School and work—teaching—were the only places in which I experienced the competence and confidence I lacked as a mother. And every day I spent at home, biting my nails in front of the television set while Joseph napped, I mapped my way back to the work and education that filled me with hope.

Sometimes, when Richard couldn't hold it in, he let his incredulity smash into me like a swatter cracking over a fly's body and only clipping its wings.

"You know, most women would kill for the opportunity to stay home with their kids. And all you want to do is avoid it. I don't get you."

What's wrong with you? I heard the last part of his statement, though he did not say it aloud. It was implied. In his tone. In the way he shook his head and wouldn't look at me. And I didn't know what was wrong with me. I just knew that something was wrong with me.

I wasn't normal. I wasn't like the mothers I met at Gymboree classes. They seemed older, self-assured, and mature. Confidence danced in the relaxed lines of their limbs as they watched their toddlers from a distance without cringing or biting their nails. They didn't appear to be on the verge of tears and helplessness when taking their kids out to the park, for God's sake. But I was different. I was crippled by the responsibility of caring for him, my ineptitude, the fear that I would kill him or scar him for life.

He became my heart, my everything, and as much as the desire to gun my engine and blast onto a highway divider burned in me—burns in me still—I pulled back on the gas every time because I knew I couldn't leave him, wouldn't let my weaknesses define his childhood, my death be his legacy to bear.

Instead, I woke up each day as if it were my last day in life, hoping for the truck that would see me at the last minute and smash into me. Of the car that would crash into my own on the way to work in the mornings, after I had deposited Joseph safely in school, taking me out of my misery. Of the student who would walk into my office one day and shoot me because he didn't receive the grade he felt he should have earned. These images, these silent hopes, were like family pictures tucked into my wallet alongside the sweet face of my son and, after Rena came, her infectious smile as well.

I braved motherhood without any tools to help me. Without a mother to guide me. I would've even taken an overbearing mother-in-law to tell me what to do. But she lived in Florida, and Richard had nothing to do with her. I only had Richard, whose role shifted from lover to father—or mother, really, his critical voice replacing Ann's in my head for the first time in our relationship—and I felt as if I'd lost my best friend, my only champion.

I stopped arguing with him. I never won. He never saw my side. He never gave in. Never apologized, even when it was obvious he was wrong. The verbal assaults were cyclical, going round and round, leaving me in this dizzying and disoriented place that Ann always abandoned me in. He became my Ann. My relationship with him morphed into the one I had with her.

There was a time in our marriage, before kids, that he argued with me until I wept out of frustration. I didn't have the skills needed to argue with someone who reveled in conflict, in having the last word, in saying whatever he needed to say to win. It was only when I cried that his voice softened. His words became disarmed, and he brought back the loving, empathetic boy I had fallen in love with.

By the time the kids came along, I realized he wanted only to worry about his work and not about how to help me solve my mothering issues. I needed him to give me permission to return to work. To know we would be okay as a couple if I placed our son in daycare. But he refused to show me compassion. I stopped crying. And without my breaking down, his kindness remained out of reach.

As soon as he began arguing, I buried my head again in the sand, in my writing, in changing diapers, in feeding toddlers, in anything that helped me avoid another long and overdrawn discussion that relegated him right and me wrong, selfish, lacking.

Richard wanted a traditional suburban marriage, but he had married an insecure feminist who only found pride in her work and her education. Mothering was not a goal of mine, a professional or personal objective. I wanted to be a mom, but not a mom buried in diapers and kin-keeping, and this became a stark difference in our roles as man and woman, husband and wife, and parents.

By the time Rena was born, I had given myself permission to place Joseph in daycare, which provided me the free time I needed to write and find part-time teaching jobs. Richard went off to work, and eventually, I learned that while he was working, he would not come to my aid if I needed his help.

His work entailed trading, and my work entailed taking care of the kids. It didn't matter that his work took him to lunch with his coworkers, or driving for hours, or going to the movies in the middle of the day. The few times I needed him to come home, or meet me at the doctor's, the answer was, "I'm at work."

I was alone. Me and my two little ones, taking first steps out into the world on trembling, ungrounded legs tripping beneath the weight of our inexperience. We learned together, holding each other's hands, crying together when we fell and skinned our knees, kissing each other's booboos. Except my booboos weren't physical or visible. They squirmed like thick, bulbous leeches beneath my skin, sucking the blood that pumped inside me until there was only blackness left. The black, smooth, fat skin of their backs, sleeping off the fatigue of their consumption.

I raised my children with this blackness, wishing it would take me away from my life.

I forced myself to stay, until that day, in my mid-forties, when Richard told me he was ready to discard me after all the years we had been together, after all the IVF treatments and the negligees and the sex I never found much pleasure in.

I had let him in—into me—into the darkness that whispered within me, and for a long time, I believed him to be the light. The one who kept me afloat, the one who would never sacrifice me as my mothers had. He had promised. That promise had disarmed me, let me fall in love with him, move in with him, and then make

a life with him until he no longer felt safe for me, and the promise
of his love became a lie.

The day I found myself on the floor, petting Morpheus's thick,
golden mane, his nose sniffing the snot on my face, I wasn't relieved that these people, strangers, found me. Preached love into
me, forgiveness. I felt defeated, my will once again overtaken by
others. I couldn't stab myself to death. I couldn't drive fast enough
to crash into a divider. And I couldn't even kill myself properly
without googling how to do it and attracting unwanted attention.
I was a hostage in my body, a hostage in my life, a hostage to
everyone else's wants.

Noticing the time, I put Richard's pills back where I found
them, climbed back into my loose-fitting shell of a body, grabbed
after-school snacks, got into my car, and drove out of my driveway to pick up my kids from school. I stepped on the gas gently,
my foot barely touching the pedal, vigilant of my left turns and
my speed.

I decided then that I would learn to carry my body with
some semblance of acceptance—if not love. Tolerance, really. I was
forced to. I would not leave my children to withstand the worst
of my failures, my inadequacies, my desire to not be. I would not
let them fall into the yawning hole I had dug for myself, breathing
in the festering rot of a life that I did not want to live. I wouldn't
be a spite ghost.

I would be practical instead. Realizing Richard was unpre-
dictable in his love for me, that I was vulnerable in my home—
not only because I wanted to kill myself but also because I had
no way of supporting myself if he left me—I updated my resume
and applied for full-time teaching jobs. Eventually, the community
college that employed me as an adjunct offered me a full-time
position. This gave me the security I needed that my marriage no
longer promised me. If he tried to divorce me, I would be ready,
armed with a job that could support me and our kids.

I put us in marriage counseling, but to no avail. The damage had been done and no apology from him, no "I love you" phrases could mend the hole he'd drilled into me that one night by telling me he didn't love me.

He tried. He bought me cards again, the way he had at the beginning, when we were in our twenties, and filled them with loving phrases. He took me to dinner without the kids in tow. He told me he hadn't meant the words that devastated me. I never told him those words had brought me to the brink of suicide.

But a door had closed inside me, and it took me a long time to understand its parameters. How deep it went, how thick and tall it stood, how unwelcome Richard would be in using it to enter the inner room I'd created to contain me, protect me from him. A year of therapy did not soften the blow of his words or the coldness that learned to live inside me.

I still fantasize about dying, about putting an end to the dark feelings crawling all over my body like maggots loosened from their cocoons, reminding me to scratch the old itch of dying and the need to disappear. But I don't take it into my own hands. I can't let this be my kids' legacy—their mother's suicide.

I don't love life, and I don't like living. If it were up to me, I wouldn't be here, taking up space. I don't like myself in this life. It's an abyss I have tripped into and cannot climb back out of. But I have made a home out of it. I find small pleasures in everyday things, like my kids, making them happy, writing, reading, teaching, my students, pursuing a PhD I don't need, applying for grants that I can add to my resume for jobs I don't apply for. I pursue these things with a biting hunger that is never quite satiated, not even when I receive publication deals for my writing or grants for my teaching.

People think I am ambitious. *Inspirational*, they write on my Facebook wall. But this is not true. I am filling up the holes, biding my time, looking the other way so I don't have to look into the gaunt face of the emptiness breathing loudly, vigorously against my skin, crawling into me through my pores. My accomplishments take up small spaces in this life that I feel forced to pretend I am grateful for. I resent it.

I resent being here, but since my body won't let go, and I can't kill it, I will wait. For cancer. For some inoperable tumor. Like the fibroid removed from my uterus last December and the hysterectomy that followed. I almost didn't come out of it. I crossed my fingers, held my children tightly, and prayed this would be it.

"You looked like death on a stick," Richard said with a laugh, when I woke up hours after they expected me to, and all I could think about was my body and how it hadn't wanted to return. It had taken its time, staying in the quiet I have yearned for, the dark place where nothing and no one exists, and yet, they'd still brought me back.

"I haven't told you this yet," I revealed to my newest therapist, a young mother of three. "But I fantasize about being in a nursing home."

"A nursing home?" she asked via video. We had to move our sessions online because of COVID-19. Therapy in self-isolation. "Because you want to be cared for?"

"Be cared for?" I repeated to myself, turning the idea around in my fingers like a Rubik's Cube with some hidden message trapped behind the mismatched colors.

"No," I said after a while. "I don't really like being taken care of. That kind of attention makes me uncomfortable. No. To be catatonic. Drugged up. I see myself retiring there, rocking in a chair, waiting to die. I just want a place to wait out life."

I watched her shift in her chair. Our time was up, and I'd just thrown a new puzzle at her.

"Well, let's talk about this next week, Marina," she told me, her brows hunched over her blue-gray eyes. "We need to think about how to make your life worth living, so you're not waiting to die."

"Sure." I reassured her with one of my wide, winning smiles. I have been taught to fool people into believing I am content. "Don't worry. I won't do anything. I'm too much of a coward for that."

"Just wait, okay? Let's talk next week." Her smile was tight and concerned.

"I'll wait," I told her. I'm good at waiting.

I wait and keep my dark thoughts to myself. No one understands that death is a longing I savor, like chocolate kisses melting on my tongue, leaving behind the memory of sweetness and a sugar rush.

I'm not afraid of dying. I'm afraid of everything that comes with living.

THE LAST TIME

*T*he last time I had sex with Richard should have been the day I left. But I didn't, for so many reasons that seem like no reasons at all when I think of them now.

It took a long time to get to Richard. To find him and trust him with my heart, my body. With my sex. He was the last boy I fell in love with and the first boy I had sex with. And for twenty-six years, twenty-two of those in our marriage, two kids, three miscarriages, a slew of dogs and cats, and two mortgage payments, he was the only man to have known me intimately. Riddled with shame and fear of sex, I made myself believe that I was destined for one man, one sexual partner, and I put all my needs into Richard. He was the one.

So, when he came upstairs to the bonus room, looked at me and said, "I want a divorce," it broke me. I felt all of me shatter and splinter like fragile glass at his feet, the shards so misshapen I didn't know how to put them back together. There were so many of them, and my hands were too shaky to try. I collected them from the floor and stuffed them back into the body Richard had once loved and touched and soothed with effortless dedication in the hopes I would make them fit again, full again.

But to no avail. No glue, no words of love or regret could put me back together.

I twisted the wedding band on my finger, the one he had inscribed with "unconditional" because he knew how important the word was to me when we tried to sort out the ways Ann had spoiled my development by not loving me back. It was a word we turned over in our fingers as if it were a snow globe full of the affection I hungered for and found only in him, sealing it in the rounded glass and holding it in the palm of my hands so I would never lose it or break it or misplace it. Aware of all the rejections by my family, he vowed before God, in church, and in front of our family and friends that he would love me unconditionally. It became our safe word.

I wore that ring for the twenty-two years I was married to him and during the first six months after I left him. Even while he took his off during the last two years of our marriage, because he gained weight, he said, I never took mine off. Not out of love, but as a reminder of how conditional love is. It had lost its original flavor, its meaning. His love did not weather all the storms in our marriage, and for many years, we were both stuck, our desire to leave each other screwed to the back of our spines to the point of paralysis, our bodies alien to each other's needs.

"Why are you still with me?" I asked him one night while in bed, me on my side and him on his, with my back to him. "I don't give you anything."

I don't clarify "anything" because we both know what I mean. I won't have sex with him. I won't kiss him. Occasionally, I will bury my body into his, just to remind myself what it's like to be touched by another human being—even this human being—but this is rare. So why does he still stick around?

"I love you, you know," he told me. I said nothing. They were just hollow words, gliding toward me and passing over my head like mosquitoes searching for a drop of blood to sustain them. I let them buzz past me and fade into the folds of the sheer curtains drawn over the window before me.

I didn't believe him. I didn't know how to make myself be-lieve him, catch the words in the palm of my hand and press them against my skin like they belonged to me, like they fit into me once more. They came too late, like Ann's words did, long after her actions proved otherwise. They no longer mattered, because too much damage had been done.

"I didn't mean it," he told me during one of our therapy sessions six months after he mentioned divorce. "I just wanted to get a reaction out of you."

"You told me you didn't love me. What reaction did you expect?"

"You know I love you," he reiterated, as if announcing it again would make me believe him.

He shook me out of my reverie, my numbness. "I don't feel anything for you, except anger" was equivalent to placing his hands on my arms and shaking me awake.

It worked. I woke up. But now I was too awake to go back to the way we used to be—comfortable with each other, tolerant of the mood swings and character inconsistencies. His rages. I was able to see him and me—us—without the veneer of love and its supposed steadfastness.

No one is obligated to love you—me—really. And everyone's love is conditional. Even mine. If he didn't love me, then I would not love him anymore. The valves which once allowed all of me to be poured into him without reservations were no longer open. They were sealed shut and cauterized, the seam barely visible. And even in my weakest moments, when I looked into his eyes and remembered the guy I used to love—especially when he was light, funny, and sweet—I didn't have the strength to unseal the vice that had been put in place to protect me from him.

One night, a year after his confession shook me and while we were still in couples therapy, he came into my office, sat in front of me, and presented himself as the boy I had discovered among many boys and fallen in love with. He showed me his kindness, his gentleness, patience, even.

"Do you want a divorce?"

I blinked, surprised by the question, so upfront and guileless.

"What? Do you?" I felt my defensiveness pulsing in rhythmic patterns, blood rushing to my cheeks.

"Sherry says when you see her in therapy, you tell her you want to be separated from me." Sherry was our couple's therapist. She saw us together and separately, and I was confident what I told her in our sessions would stay between us. I was wrong.

"I don't know. Sometimes."

Richard took my hands and placed them inside his. I loved his hands. His fingers were long and strong, with the right amount of red-gold hair sprouting from the knucklebones.

"If you want to divorce me, it's okay. I'll do whatever you want. If you want to stay here, I will move out. If you want to move out, I will help you. I only want you to be happy."

There was something stuck in my throat that made it hard for me to speak. I kept the truth in there. I was unhappy. I fantasized about moving out daily, getting my own apartment, having the kids, then eight and four, every other week, parenting without Richard's undermining in sight, being a mother and myself all at the same time. On my own terms.

This is what I told Sherry. I felt trapped. In silences. In words I was too afraid to speak into the air lest someone heard them, making me unable to put them back into the jar that kept them sealed.

"Think about it," he said and went back upstairs to read a book to our daughter.

The entire time he was talking to me, my eyes kept going to one place: the staircase. There were two portraits set up against the wall alongside each other. One was of our daughter when she was three, her red, curly hair glistening in the sunlight, and the other was of our son, when he was three — four years apart — his gaze wide and thoughtful. The word divorce juxtaposed harshly against these two images of my small children, helpless, still blank slates of potential. What would a divorce do to them?

I remember when my father left. How his leaving was a life-saving decision for him that had taken him away from his wife's abusive fists and kicks. But in saving himself, he had abandoned us—his kids. Without him, my mother did not work and couldn't keep her children. He didn't take us with him because he moved in with his older sister, who had no room for his four kids. She was taking care of her brother, her husband, and his ailing mother. My brothers were placed in orphanages, raised by strangers until they were eighteen. And my sister and I spent a few years with our mother—the worst years—when girls first learn about girl-hood, except ours were entrenched in sex work, homelessness, and violence.

All of this occurred when one parent left. My entire childhood shifted and fragmented and forced me and my siblings into pre-carious and unsafe corners of life opposite one another, corners we are each trying to overcome—still—now in our early fifties. Knowing what happens when one parent leaves—how could I leave? I couldn't. I wouldn't be the one to leave. I can only be left. Abandoned. I'm used to it.

I didn't leave then. I should have. But I didn't. And that is on me.

I went to bed that night, the images of my children at three years old still fresh in my mind, their innocence in my hands, in my choices, and I chose to stay.

"I don't want a divorce," I told Richard, moving closer to him, pulling his face close to mine, planting my mouth on his, suckling the desire to separate or divorce out of his mouth and pulling it into my own. Swallowing it. Ingesting it so that it trav-eled to the low, acid-filled recesses of my stomach, undigested, circling with impatience, burning into me, moving up into my abdomen, my chest, its sour-tasting acid backing up into my mouth like the words I keep trapped there and won't let out. Heartburn.

We made love that night, and while our bodies went through the motions of entanglement and love and commitment to stay together, I couldn't stop thinking this was the first time I was having sex with him because I wanted to make it all okay. To appease him. To pacify the doubts in his mind—and mine. To keep everything the same.

I always had one rule about sex. I would never have it if I didn't want it. I would never participate in sex if it blurred with some other need, like taking away Richard's hurt, or shutting him up during a fight, or getting something I wanted or needed. Transactional sex, like the sex my birth mother modeled for me, for money or chicken or a roof over her head. And until that night, I never did. No matter how much Richard wanted to have sex, I refused to be intimate with him unless it was also something I wanted. If I was not in the mood, it didn't happen. Ever.

But that night, I wasn't so sure. The sex we had felt forced, manipulated. A reassurance we would be okay. Sex to seal the deal. A promise to stay together. And for someone like me—with my history with sex, my fear of it, my fear of its corruptive forces, its power to blur agency and truth—for the first time in my life as a sexual being, I believed I was having sex to save my marriage. My sex, this one time, was compromised. I was compromised.

I haven't been able to shake off this truth, this one blurring line which has tainted my resolve to always have agency when it came to sex.

I was like everyone else—like the women I know who have confessed that they lie beneath their husbands because it's Thursday—sex day—or because he wants it or might go elsewhere if she doesn't give it to him, like candy or an allowance. Or because he has a stressful job or is angry or has OCD, and he looks to her sex as a benefit, a temporary relief.

Better yet, like my birth mother, for whom sex was like lying on a conveyor belt, her body surrendering, giving itself away to get something in return.

Quid pro quo is the term I use when teaching my women's studies courses. Transactional sex. Like her, I'd had sex for a reason—and this reason wasn't desire or passion or love. It was desperation. I felt dirty, dishonest. I still do, thinking about it now. It was like taking money from him. Trading sex for security.

I've not told anyone. Until now. To you, reading my words, my confession, for the first time in over a decade. That is how shameful it was for me to have transactional sex with my husband that night. And I vowed it would never happen again.

"I don't want to have sex anymore," I told him in front of our therapist while in counseling several days later.

"What?" He leaned forward, casting a sharp look in my direction that said, *you're ridiculous*. The heel of his foot was tapping on the floor, the only sound vibrating between our pauses. "Ever?"

"No. I'm done with that part of my life. I want to work, live our lives and raise our children together as partners, but I don't want to have sex anymore."

My chin jutted out, and I could feel my lips draw into a tight line across my face. The deafening sound of my heartbeat thrummed in my ears the way the ocean sounds, deep and throbbing, when you put your ear to the opening canal of a conch shell.

I wasn't sure I could demand such a thing: a marriage without sex, without intimacy. But here I was, asking permission. And I was asking. Hoping, really. I didn't know if I could demand it.

"But what about Richard?" asked Sherry, our middle-aged therapist from the South.

"What about him?" I heard the coldness in my voice before I could contain it.

"Well, how is that being fair to him?" I tossed Sherry an incredulous look. Her question reminded me of the time I'd told a friend I didn't shave my legs. Not only because of my feminism and my resistance to my body's feminization, but also because my hair was dark and thick, which required me to shave every day. It's tedious and time-consuming, and I hate primping myself so my body can be acceptable by society's standards.

My friend's immediate response was, "Poor Richard. How does he feel about that?" Since when did women's bodies and the choices we make for our bodies become a burden for men?

Taking a deep breath, I rested my gaze on Richard, who sat opposite me in a chair he rocked back and forth, his leg shaking out his frustration. I knew I had thrown him off, but this was not something I could say to him outside of this office. I couldn't explain it to him well enough, and he wouldn't understand. We had lost the ability to speak to one another and be understood. I'd forgotten how to talk to him. I'd lost the courage it took to speak from my heart.

"How is it fair to me to have sex with him when I don't want to?"

"You're not being fair to yourself either," our therapist pointed out, her red hair bobbing up and down as she tried to find the right words for our situation. "Sex is a natural human condition. You're depriving yourself of pleasure and intimacy."

"I'd rather have a different kind of intimacy. Intimacy of the mind and of raising our children together. Just not the touching stuff."

I felt like a little girl, cornered, unable to make the adults around me understand how it felt having transactional sex with my husband. How dirty it all made me feel in places that didn't see light or hope. The places of my childhood, still buried, forced to take long, arduous breaths through cracks in sealed crates.

Being touched by men's hands always felt dirty to me. I'd scrubbed the memory of their fingers off my skin with soap in my twenties. And although Richard's hands were never rough or gross, his touch became something I felt the need to disavow, and I didn't know how to stop it. His touching or my response to his touch. Both felt unnatural to me, and I couldn't locate the words needed to convey this.

In retrospect, my desire to avoid intimacy with Richard had much to do with three events: his telling me he didn't love me, my attempt to kill myself because of it, and our having transactional sex as a cure-all for our problems. They had triggered me, and my response had been to stay in my marriage for my kids but to withdraw from him, the source of my pain. To protect myself, really.

"You're doing this to punish me," he raised his voice, leaning forward in his chair opposite my own.

"To punish you for what?" I asked.

"For telling you I don't love you. For telling you I want a divorce."

I sat back in my chair and looked at him with a blank expression on my face.

"I'm not trying to punish you. I don't want to have sex. Period. With anyone. Ever again. I want complete control over my body. I want nothing to go into it and nothing to come out of it. I want to move on without any of it."

I didn't know how else to be clear. I wasn't trying to punish him or hurt him. I was only trying to protect myself—the way I learned to protect myself before I met him, before the day he sauntered into my life and dared me to love, to touch and be touched, to give a voice and a life to my desires.

He gave, and then he took away.

And I gave until there was nothing more to give.

Nothing but fear and unhappiness and an ache that keeps my fingers frozen on my lap without a desire to touch or be touched.

We stayed together, lying next to each other on the same

bed, angry or not, ambivalent or not, joking or not. We didn't talk the way we used to, delving into long conversations until dawn's light beckoned us to rise from the sunken mattress that had memorized our shapes, side-by-side, weight by weight during the decades we shared together.

But that was the last time we had sex. The last time I believed I would ever have sex.

I remained unsexed for the remaining ten years that my marriage to Richard lasted. And despite the pitiful looks I received from women to whom I said this aloud, I felt liberated. In control of myself, my body, and my life. There was clarity in not having sex. You knew where everyone and everything belonged, and there was no confusion, no veneer, no room for betrayal. There was safety in owning my body in marriage—especially one that no longer functioned out of love or respect.

For the first time in years, I was comfortable in my skin, in my body. Because it belonged to me and me alone. I didn't have to share it with anyone. I didn't have to lie beneath another body and pretend sex was normal, sex was good, or sex was what I wanted—especially with a man who had decided he no longer loved me—or could use my love to control me, to get me to act the way he wanted and expected.

Because I don't think I have ever wanted sex.

I have only ever wanted to be loved.

And without his love, there could be no sex. Not for me. Not back then. Not when I, and my body, no longer trusted his words, his feelings, or his actions. In becoming unsexed, I gave myself permission to live my life for me, on my terms, even while staying married for the sake of my children.

I was too afraid to leave him, to be on my own, but unsexed, my body kept me safe in a marriage that no longer felt safe or good or kind.

PTSD AND
(M)OTHERHOOD

*W*hen Joseph was still little, around four, I remember taking him to a Barnes & Noble bookstore back in New York. I didn't go for any specific reason other than to take Joseph out of the house, to tire him out before naptime, but I ended up in the psychology section of the store. My eyes caught sight of books on post-traumatic stress disorder. I took a workbook from the stacks, sat down on the floor next to my son's stroller, placed a handful of Cheerios on his tray for him to munch on, and then threw myself into the symptoms for PTSD.

I always knew I had PTSD but had never done much about it. The first therapist I saw was with Richard, after we were engaged, because I wanted us to enter marriage without our childhood baggage. Obviously, it didn't help.

But Lynn was not a very good therapist. She became more of a friend to us, and at the end of our sessions, we knew more about her than we did about what made us tick. We were with her until we got married and then we gave up on her when her own marriage began falling apart, and our sessions became intermittent.

I had a few individual sessions with another therapist, this time a psychologist, but she was too abrasive for me. When I told her I used to have temper tantrums as a child, she told me my mother had a right to treat me as she did. I was having a tantrum. But she didn't ask why, and she didn't appear to care about the most traumatic parts of my childhood. When I told her I wasn't on birth control, she accused me of wanting to get pregnant. When I told her we got a puppy, she accused me of sabotaging myself.

The most powerful thing she said to me was, "It sounds to me like you're treading water. You can't tread water your whole life."

These were good observations that should have prevented me from becoming a ghost in my own life, leaving Richard to make all the decisions for us because I was too insecure, but she didn't wade gently into discussions with me. She bolted me to the floor with judgments, and after three sessions, I was too intimidated to return to therapy. To return to her. I fled and disappeared into my messy mothering and family life. With no life vest to keep me above water, I continued dog-paddling out of desperation, even though I was afraid of swimming unless my feet could touch bottom.

So there I was, in my mid-thirties, curled up in the psychology section of a local Barnes & Noble store, trying to figure my own way out of pain by checking off the signs for PTSD.

I found myself there because day in and day out, I was all alone. I was married, yes. I was a new mother, yes. But I had no one to help me with my new role as a mother, and a new personality was growing like a virus beneath my usually calm and controlled demeanor.

I raised my son with tears on my face, often leaving him seated in front of the television set so I could go into the backyard and scream as if I needed to release a glob of gas burgeoning from indigestion. When I returned to the living room, my son's eyes flung back to *SpongeBob SquarePants*, pretending he hadn't seen, hadn't heard his mother act like a child.

He and I were like siblings, growing up together, finding our footing at the same time, releasing our frustration in tantrums that left us bashing our fists against the floor and weeping for relief and understanding. I was there to console him, day in and day out, with no one to console me. I was all alone with only a toddler present, watchful, and dependent on me to figure it all out. But I was as helpless as he was.

I turned the page and took notes in the small journal I carried around in my purse, mostly to jot down Joseph's milestones. The first word, the first tooth, the first time he almost drowned in my care, or the first time he slipped in the tub, blood gushing from his mouth and mixing with his bathwater. The many times I failed to snatch him from harm or overreacted to his whines by howling into my own curled fists while tucked into the bathroom, so he couldn't see or hear me.

PTSD was a homemade bomb strapped to my chest with someone else's thumb on the trigger, not knowing when the next cry from my son or my next failing would surge through me like a ripple of shockwaves from the explosion and fling me back to the wars of my childhood.

I learned that post-traumatic stress disorder occurs in the reptilian part of the brain, which is responsible for survival and automatic body responses. Without trauma, your brain responds to occurrences in a neutral state; however, with trauma, your brain switches to survival mode in which the reactive parts of your brain take over. While your body prepares for fight or flight, you have little control over what you do because the reptilian part of your brain takes over and keeps you in a reactive state.

This is me. All the time. I am always in a reactive state, hypervigilant, and this is exhausting, both emotionally and physically.

There are multiple signs of PTSD, and the ones I encounter include flashbacks, constant anxiety, avoidance of people or places that remind me of traumatic events, a sense of constant unhappiness, loss of interest in life, feeling emotionally numb or detached, and memory loss.

Sitting next to my son, reading this book, I felt acknowledged for the first time since I became a mother. All my symptoms and all the rage that burned in me were in that workbook, and I hadn't been imagining it. There was something wrong with me. There is something wrong with me. The anger living in me surfaced like a savage dog and found its way in through trauma.

When we moved to North Carolina, we lived in a lovely, wooded area among the rest of middle-class America. I blended in as a wife and the mother of two kids, picking up after a dog who trotted along the perimeter of our wrought-iron fence, barking indiscriminately at squirrels and passersby. I was employed, educated, and I chauffeured my kids from school to Tae Kwon Do to ballet to piano to soccer. But my most important job was to keep the dark shadows of my childhood at bay, ensuring none of them touched the calm life I had built for myself and those I loved.

At night, when they were all fast asleep, I paced along the edges of my anxieties and fears like a guard dog, protecting my children from the post-traumatic stress disorder simmering beneath my domesticated veneer. I couldn't always control its comings and goings; it slithered out when I least expected it and interfered with the life I had built and the children I was attempting to raise in a healthy way.

Like most post-traumatic stress casualties, I was often stuck in my memories, reliving them in my thoughts, my feelings, and in the few images I held onto from my childhood. I disappeared into these images, these memories, so much so that I shut out the noises and voices of my present surroundings. My kids woke me up with screams when they were fighting, or by shoving my arm to rouse me. Richard didn't understand how I could disappear into my own thoughts while surrounded by him, by my kids, by the noises of daily life.

It was easy, really. It's still easy. It's like nothing else exists when I enter the private sector of my mind. This is called social withdrawal. My body is present, and I smile and nod my head as if I am listening, but really, I'm not even there. I have taught myself to disappear.

Although PTSD is often associated with war veterans, one need not be entrenched in a war to suffer the symptoms. Of course, it wasn't until the feminists of the 1960s and 1970s advocated for abused women and children that our understanding of the disorder was expanded wide enough to include those who had suffered traumatic experiences not associated with war.

Like women.

The problem with women suffering from post-traumatic stress disorder is they become mothers, like me, like my birth mother, who live in a home with children, and since the primary care of children falls on the mother, this becomes a tenuous situation. There is no doubt in my mind that my birth mother suffered from post-traumatic stress disorder, for when I met her again in my thirties, twenty years after I was removed from her negligent care, she disassociated from her own experiences, talking about herself in the third person as if the woman who loved my father and gave birth to his children had not been her but another woman, another prostitute.

As self-aware as I am, as I thought I was, I waltzed into marriage and motherhood with my eyes half open, not realizing how my own experiences with sexual corruption and violence would degrade my maternal intentions. With as much love and affection as I cloaked my children's lives, my aims were spotty, spoiled by either emotional detachment or outbursts that left my children aching.

Women with PTSD exhibit symptoms that include intensity, isolation, passivity, anger, and feelings of powerlessness and weakness. It is no wonder that when my children were small, I was kicking garbage cans, slamming doors and cabinets, and screaming at the top of my lungs in the same way my birth mother bellowed her own inarticulate frustrations when I had been her child. This is called vicarious or secondary traumatization, and it describes a process by which children adopt or mimic their parents' trauma-related symptoms.

When my son was little, he used to knock his head against floors and walls out of frustration. Leaping forward to cradle his head in my hands before it met another firm surface, I often wondered if that was his reaction to me. If it was all me. Even though I did not dare touch them when angry, my children lost a bit of their innocence each time they experienced the dark side of my mothering. Instead of security and safety, they discovered in me a trauma they had not experienced, and one which they may also enact when they are older, in front of their own children.

Post-traumatic stress disorder ripples through time, beginning with my mother, who witnessed the abuse of her mother, trickling into me, and finding roots in my own children like a ceaseless stream of water without a beginning or an end in sight. It merely flows forward, gathering and dragging sediments of its past and present travails with exhausting force. I often wonder how it will present itself to my own children. What they will remember and how the blame will rest on me.

Because of this, I walked on eggshells in my home, not knowing how I would react when my son accidentally hit me while chasing the dog, or when my daughter tickled me in places I found uncomfortable, like my neck or my chest; or when my husband crawled into bed and I instinctively reached for the edges of the mattress, my back to him, tucked into myself like a roly-poly out of fear he would touch me, want sex from me. Because anyone's hands on me make me retreat into myself—even the hands belonging to those I love.

The night that Richard faced me and told me he wanted a divorce triggered my PTSD. His words, his rejection of me opened an old wound that he and I covered up with a Band-Aid, applied by two hurt people who believed unconditional love would save us. It never really healed. It was just hidden, still struggling for breath beneath a cloak of despair, waiting for the love to fade, the lies to unearth themselves, the veneer of healing and being healed wiped from the surface of my body and life as if it were collecting dust on an old, tattered oak table in the corner of an abandoned room, unused and uncared for.

I was walking around with an open and infected wound, and everything that touched its raw nerves left its mark on it, corroding any opportunities of healing. Anything that touched that open wound left me reeling and raw.

Like the night Richard came into the bonus room as I was watching *Columbo* and thrust his iPhone at me, showing me a video that had just gone viral. Within the first few seconds of the video, I saw a man standing opposite an eight-year-old girl. Her back to the camera, she had short brown hair swishing against her naked back. She wasn't wearing a shirt.

The video was of Judge William Adams beating his daughter, which had been posted on YouTube. But I hadn't gotten to that part yet. I was still transfixed by the image of a man, fully dressed, standing in a room with a half-naked little girl, and the quiet sounds of their movements.

It was the quiet that triggered me. Her bare back, the spinal cord protruding from beneath her skin, her little body standing there, still and hushed, the only sounds coming from the man moving about. His muscles contracting, his bones creaking, his pants creasing about his thighs as he stepped closer to the girl. It was the quiet that burned into me like a lit cigarette being twisted against the inside of my wrist, leaving a scorched, aching hole behind.

"Turn it off! Turn it off!" I screamed at Richard, shoving the phone back at him. I placed my hands over my ears, shut my eyes, rolled into a fetal ball at the corner of the couch, and rocked back and forth, trying to erase the image of the girl's bare skin and the sounds of her screams.

Richard looked at me with a peculiar expression on his face from the distance I imposed between us. In all the years he had known me, he had never seen me transported to this dark and childlike state. Maybe the quiet room, the sound of the man's movements in that silence, and the bare back of the girl reminded me of Mr. Schwartz. Or maybe it all reminded me of Kristos, or of the orphanage. Whatever it was, I had been triggered.

When I tried to recount the incident to my therapist later in the week, I became mute, my mouth opening and closing without words to utter. Just guttural spasms. In describing the scene and my reaction, my voice went hoarse and then disappeared. Rendered silent, my physical response revealed more than any words could: tears streamed down my cheeks, my hands trembled on my lap, my heart banged against the walls of my chest, and my body felt completely disconnected from me and my surroundings.

My therapist put her notebook down, looked directly at me, and said, "You have PTSD."

I already knew this, but it was the first time a professional had confirmed it.

I wept in her office that day because someone had finally seen the parts of me that needed to be acknowledged. It's like telling people you see ghosts, but no one believes you until the day they see them, too.

It's reaffirming when someone else is a witness to your ghosts. In seeing them, they finally see you.

ELEVEN BODIES

"I've only had eleven bodies," my son told me one day as we were discussing his online dating sex-capades.

We were in the kitchen, and I was preparing eggs and toast for him. Because he asked. Joseph came out of the dark cave in his room and asked me to feed him. A rare occurrence in his seventeen years.

"Eleven bodies?" I asked, throwing a quizzical glance at his smiling face.

"Yeah," he nodded his head. "You know, I've had sex with eleven bodies."

"Joseph," I began in my women's studies professorial tone. "They're not bodies. They're people. Boys. They have names, identities, histories. When you refer to them as bodies, you take all of those away. You objectify them."

"I know, Mom. But it's different for our generation. We don't put such importance on sex."

"It's not the sex that is the problem. It's the fact that you treat each other like vacant bodies, existing solely for physical pleasure. It would be so much better if you got to know each other. Cared for each other. Didn't treat each other like *things*."

He rolled his eyes at me, and I tried to find new ways to articulate to him the need for intimacy and connection outside of body-to-body fucking that had become his way to connect with other boys his age.

Joseph had been baptized into gay sex by the dangerous seawaters of Grinder, an adult app for gay men and boys. You had to be eighteen to engage, but he lied about his age, and the men on the site ignored his youthful looks.

We were in Greece when he lost his virginity, leaving our hotel room in the morning, saying he was going for a walk to talk to his friends on the phone. What we didn't know was that he had downloaded Grinder and gone to a nearby hotel to meet up with a man who showed interest in him.

Months later, we discovered the app on his phone and grounded him from internet and social media usage, only to discover from his texts that the man he had gone to meet up with also had a partner in that hotel room. Apparently, it's a thing for older men to go on the app and find young boys to initiate into sex. The men were in their mid- to late-thirties. Joseph was only sixteen.

I think back on that day, the way Richard called him and demanded that he return to the hotel room after realizing that he was up to no good; the way Joseph went straight to the bathroom to brush his teeth for the umpteenth time, from oral sex, Richard told me. I was clueless.

"Yeah, go explore the city. I used to do it as a kid, too, when I traveled with my mom," had been my nonchalant response. It never occurred to me he was impulsive enough to push through fear to get to the excitement of having sex for the first time, with a stranger, in a foreign country, where being gay was an open and acceptable concept.

"Mom, this is nothing new. This is how most gay guys have sex. Did you think I would find a nice gay kid at a Catholic school in the South to date and then make love to?"

Yes. I nodded my head. "Why not? You're a nice gay kid going to a Catholic school in the South. You're not the only one. Maybe they haven't come out yet, but they do exist."

Despite the grounding and social media limits, Joseph found ways through which to explore his newfound interest in sex. He had Snapchat and found gay boys there. His age, he told me. His age, I hoped. I never know what the truth is with Joseph. He lies, and I am not good at figuring out which words he says are lies and which ones aren't. I am more concerned with why he lies.

I know it's because he has been living a double life. Hiding his gayness while attending Catholic school since kindergarten, taking mandatory theology classes with teachers who called gay men and women aberrations, ungodly, dirty, and vile. Their words.

But Joseph is none of those things. He is the kindest soul, with empathy rolling over him in full, luscious green patches of healthy grass covering up the wounds and hurts our hetero-normative and conservative society, schools, and home kept bashing against his head until he felt powerless and confused.

Richard and I were part of the problem. We raised him straight. We assumed he was straight, like most parents do with their kids. Richard talked to him about girls and erections and masturbation. I talked to him about girls and sex and consent. The kids at his school didn't talk to him at all, because he was not a "boy's boy." The porn industry defined gay sex for him, showed him who he was, the type of sex that turned him on, and the various skills he needed to have oral sex, anal sex, and everything in between. Lessons on human objectification come from this industry, whether you are gay, bi, or straight.

He snuck out of the house at night, picked up by boys he met online, and disappeared for a few hours. It took a while for me to figure out what he was doing.

"Why are you sneaking out?" I asked him. "You're putting yourself in danger."

A shrug noted I wouldn't understand. I'm a mom. I'm straight. I've only been with one man. What would I know about his needs, gay needs? Gay sex, for that matter.

"All I'm trying to say, Joseph, is that you don't need to sneak out of the house. We know you're gay. We know you're sexually active, albeit I don't know if you're having safe sex. They can pick you up in the evening, like normal people, take you out, and then bring you back here."

"I'm gay, Mom. In the South. I can't walk out in the middle of the day with another guy, a Black guy, mind you, hold his hand and kiss him if I wanted. Trust me. I've tried."

I nodded. They had to meet up in the dark, have sex in the darkest parts of an abandoned parking lot, in his car, or someone else's car. The South was not only homophobic but also racist.

I ran my gaze over him as if it were my hands, stroking away the pain we instilled in him by forcing him to live a double life—one in the light and one in the dark. The one in the dark was his life, the one that spoke to him, called to him, knew his secret, and refused to name it to the world.

I think of myself when I was young. I met boys at clubs, made out with them, and gave them my number. If they called, we went out on a date, made out in the car some more. But I didn't have sex with them. And I was nineteen or twenty. I know I can't compare myself to him. I had sex for the first time when I was twenty-five, and even then, it was with the man I knew I was going to marry. Growing up in the eighties and nineties was also different than it is now. We didn't have computers or iPhones or dating apps, and when we met prospective romantic partners, we met them face-to-face. There's something to be said about that.

I wonder what sex is like for him. If it's reciprocated or if he's the one on his knees during these dates, giving without receiving. I want to broach the subject, but I also want to respect his privacy.

I'm scared. All the time. About his well-being, his physical and emotional safety.

I want to be there for him the way Ann wasn't there for me. She never spoke to me about sex other than to call me a whore or tell me that blow jobs were "disgusting." Richard taught me about sex. He taught me how to masturbate. The men in my childhood taught me the dangers that came with sex, with lust, with male desire.

I would rather a woman had taught me about sex. A parent who balanced caution with the realities of sex and love. But since Ann had none of these experiences herself and did not offer them to me as drops of wisdom one shares with her child, I was always on my own.

I don't want my kids to be on their own. To be independent, yes. To learn from their own mistakes, yes. But not to feel like they exist without arms and legs and stomachs to cushion their falls when they learn about the hardships that come with living.

When he was still in high school, I considered sneaking into my son's phone and reading his messages. Putting a tracker in his car. Following him on these dates. Cock-blocking him is the term used these days. This would have made me feel better. I would have known where he was. I would have been privy to his experiences, and when he walked past me and went to his room, I wouldn't have to wait for him to come to me when he was ready to talk, giving me scraps of information like single drops of water escaping from a faulty faucet. I would know everything that had occurred around that drop, all the details, and I would plan a conversation about the issues I thought were important.

But I knew this was wrong. As wrong as when Ann locked me out of the apartment whenever I returned home from a nightclub or a date between the ages of nineteen and twenty-four. I smacked the palm of my hand against the wooden door for her to let me in.

"You woke me," she told me as she turned the lock on the deadbolt and pried the chain from the door.

"Well, if you didn't lock me out, I would come in without waking you."

She blocked me so that upon entering the apartment, I couldn't walk around her and go to my room. I had only one direction to enter and move into. The salon. The living room. I sat on the blue floral couch I had known since my adoption at eight and waited for her to conduct her ritual.

She sat opposite me and watched me without saying a word. Her brown eyes examined my body for evidence of my corruption, my whorishness, my resemblance to my birth mother. Was my lipstick smeared? Were my pupils dilated? Did I slur my words? Were my buttons intact? Did I look disheveled, as if I had been tussling in the back seat of a car with a boy?

I had every right to these things in my twenties, but since I still lived with her, I had to obey her rules. And this was her rule for going out and coming home late. I had to be surveyed for drugs, sex, and alcohol.

Nothing else mattered to her. Not that I was in graduate school with a 4.0 GPA, that I worked two jobs to pay for my college tuition, or that I was the only twenty-something-year-old virgin I knew. All that mattered was that my body was not sullied by my poor choices. Not that she knew anything about my body. How much I loved and hated it. How much I protected it from being pried open by male hands and eyes. She only saw that it was wasted, old, hunched, fatigued, defiled. And it was all those things, but that was, according to her, my doing, not hers.

Richard and I had to untie all the knots inside of Joseph once he came out to us. We had to unlearn everything as well. What did we know about raising a gay son? Nothing.

There is fragility in my son's long, lanky physique. He's tall and thin without an ounce of fat on him, his ribs protruding from beneath his skin, his gut gaunt. There's a vulnerability in his eyes, in his smile, when he chooses to smile. He takes all of it in, but it's like he's not there. He sits at the kitchen table for dinner as we take turns reciting our favorite and worst parts of the day, and he participates without being present. He doesn't belong, doesn't want to belong to us, to be part of this family. And this could be the teenage angst in him, but it could be more.

I don't know because he's a lot like me. Watching, waiting to disappear back into his room where he has his social network in various apps on his phone and the disembodied voices of his gaming buddies talking to him from the Xbox.

He looked at me one day, during dinner. We were rehashing childhood memories. Rena started it.

"Do you remember the time you chased me, and I fell and got that scar on my back?" she asked him, half-accusing, half-laughing. I can see the scar between her shoulder blades even now, her back away from me, her shirt concealing the stark, white line that becomes brighter when the skin around it grows darker each summer when she tans.

"Yeah," he chuckled, dragging his long fingers along the thick mass of brown, almost jet-black hair that sits like a crown atop his head.

"Remember when you fell in the pool and no one heard you fall in?" he asked her, shaking his head.

"You saved my life," she smiled at him, and I followed by recounting the traumatic experience of having our backs turned as she ran around the pool and fell in without making a splash or letting out a scream.

It was Joseph who screamed: "Rena fell in the pool!" Richard jumped in and pulled her up, pushing her through the surface of the water, both drenched, smelling of chlorine and trepidation.

"Yeah," I chimed in. "Rena slammed her head into car side mirrors and fell downstairs because she always ran without paying attention to her surroundings."

"You," I continued, looking at Joseph. "You used to throw yourself on the ground and bang your head against it. Even against walls, at times. I was always rushing toward you with my hands outstretched to cushion your head. It was so scary."

I sighed, remembering the days I mothered him without resources or advice, falling on my face in learning how to care for him alone from day to day, crying myself to sleep because every day was a struggle that tested my competence as a mother, every bruise on his flesh and chipped tooth in his mouth a stone lodged in the back of my throat, reminding me of my failures.

That's when he looked at me, his eyes resting on me as if a thought had trapped him there. It was a long gaze, one in which I was allowed to gaze back, unsure of what thoughts lay in it, behind the hazel eyes he inherited from his father.

"What?" I asked him. "Why are you looking at me?"

He shook his head, unaware that he had lingered. A pang of guilt rose to my cheeks. Did I say something wrong? Did I reveal something about his childhood that was a revelation to him?

He is too much like me in this, comfortable living in a world that exists solely in him, only a visitor to this one—where I sat and waited for him to come to me, to ask me a question, to invite me in. My body vibrated with agitation, with the desire for him to reveal to me who he was and what he was thinking.

"Are you okay?" I asked when entering his room to offer him a plate of sliced peaches for a snack. "Are you happy?"

"Yeah," he said, his fingers tugging at the joystick, his earphones pushed away from one ear so he could hear me.

"Are you happy?" He returned the question, his eyes on me for a few seconds before reverting to the violence on the blue screen attached to his wall.

"Yeah," I said, wrapping my smile around his bones in the hopes he felt the adoration I always hold for him. I wondered if he was happy. His words said he was, but nothing in his body—covered in sweats and sweatshirts even in the summer months, concealed in the dark corners of his room—echoed happiness. His smiles were as empty as his words. As empty as mine.

So much fear lives in me for him. My body trembles with it, and it takes so much effort for me to comfort and quiet the tremors, hypervigilance bolting me to the ground with spike nails hammered through every single one of my toes. Only my body detects the voice that echoes of dangers, agitation spreading into my own thoughts like the stench of dead fish. A stench I can't scrub off, no matter how much water and soap I use. I, in turn, share my phobias, putrid and vile, with the members of my family, because fear has its own heartbeat, a life of its own, throbbing like a virus that consumes, ravenous with destruction.

"You could be raped," I warned him when he attempted to go on another date with a boy he talked to on some teen app. I was thinking about all the gay boys who have sat in my office or classroom, confessing to me, their teacher, a stranger—not their parents, not their family—that they are gay. Confessing the times they were raped—as boys, as young men, on dates, by family or community members they trusted. They're gay boys, straight boys, trans boys, Black boys, white boys, Asian boys, but their stories chant the same narrative. They are as prevalent as the stories I hear from the girls who come into my office, close the door, and weep about their own sexual assaults.

Rapists don't discriminate. They look for innocence, goodness, easy, unadulterated laughter, and they go in for the kill, snuffing out the light that used to live there, in their once lithe, athletic, and confident bodies. Now their spines are curled, their laughter is short-lived, and their bodies house the assaults with walls of silent forbearance. A house, a body full of shame and inarticulate pain.

I let them unload on me because I can take it. I can carry

their pain. I know what it's like to be silenced, to be abused, to be torn apart by the wants of others. I can't heal them, but I can take it, because they have no one else to talk to. And I am there.

"Don't be ridiculous," Joseph told me, putting on his jacket, grabbing his keys, his towering, lanky figure sauntering toward the front door. He was thinking about the next few hours of wooing, the sex in the back seat of the car, the blow jobs, the excitement of being with a new guy he's only talked to with a phone screen cast between them.

I don't like this world of promiscuity, of open sex and one-night stands. It's precarious. He snowballs into the waters of a lifestyle I spent my lifetime avoiding. And fearing. He jumps in with both feet, laughing, free and unencumbered by anxiety.

"I'm meeting up with him for sex. How can I be raped if it's consensual?"

"You don't know these guys. They could be haters, homophobes, luring you to an isolated spot just to attack you. You don't know. That's the point. Why can't you meet someone first, face-to-face, ask them out, go on a date, and then have sex? There's a process that needs to take place. What you're doing is dangerous." I wanted to grab his arm, force him into his room for a time-out, as I used to when he was little. Actually, he used to put himself in time-out when he knew he'd done something wrong. I wished he would do that again, at the age of seventeen and eighteen and nineteen.

When he came home from a date, he nodded, climbed the stairs, went to his room, locked the door. After a few minutes, I could hear him yelling like a child while playing *Fortnite* with his friend Tyler, who lives in Wisconsin. He is Joseph's constant friend, the only one, really, but they have never met in a physical space.

Eventually, my son was raped. He got into a car with the wrong guy. One who masked his predatory nature by wearing red Mickey Mouse pajamas and spiked Joseph's Cookout drink with a date rape drug.

What was the reason for the rape, the drink spike? Joseph would have had sex with him, anyway. But rape is about access, power, doing what you want with someone's body while pretending they don't inhabit it. How do you teach that to a young boy? My childhood and my professional background readied me to teach my daughter about rape, but I never considered applying it to my son.

Joseph's body is just a body, someone else's eleventh or twenty-sixth body—his identity, his kindness, his eternal sweetness erased, muted out of him. Sex now is as hard for him as it was for me growing up. Worse, actually. Because of my experiences with my birth mother and the time I spent in the orphanage, I muted my sexuality so that no one could find it. I only let it out when I was ready, and it didn't exist unless I told it to. I had control over my body, my desires, and who was given access to it. Joseph's exposure to sex from porn didn't teach him about rape. It only showed him men having consensual sex.

He hadn't grown up around my mother, a sex worker, to understand that even when paying for it, men could rape, and beat, and leave a body disconnected from its person. I did. I watched it. And I took notes to make sure it didn't happen to me. But I didn't take good enough notes to ensure it wouldn't happen to my son. Not my gay son. Not my sweet boy, who is triggered and traumatized in ways I will never know or understand deeply enough to help him heal his wounds.

"Are you ever suicidal?" I asked him recently, after he told me he'd hooked up with a guy at college and froze during sex. The next day, he broke down at work, and his boss walked him to the campus counseling center where he unloaded his life's burdens.

He's only nineteen. His life has just begun, really, and it's already warped and disfigured. Mangled beyond recognition by rapists and body counting and the porn industry and religious institutions that tell him he is invisible, an outcast who can never be touched by God's light. If there even is a God.

"I knew you were going to ask me that!" He laughed and turned his body so he could look at me while I drove him from campus to my apartment for the summer break.

"After the incident with the guy, when I froze, but he kept going, I did. I wanted to kill myself, Mom."

I paused, holding my breath for a second or two.

"And what made you not do it?" I struggled with the wording, but this is how it came out. Not perfect, but perfectly clear.

"You." Now he paused. "I knew that if I killed myself, then you would kill yourself, and then that would screw up Rena's life forever. So you and Rena. You made me not do it."

I caught my breath then, at that moment, and felt tears collecting in my eyes.

How did he know? How did he know that without him in this world, I would not want to stay in it? Without his light, I would be cast in the full force of darkness that lives and has always lived in me. That without him and his sister, there would be nothing. Not for me. He keeps me here, and it seems I keep him here, too. We are each other's anchor, holding us here, by force, by obligation. Even by love.

I wonder how much of me and the blackness that breathes inside me he has learned from me because he has been watching and listening and taking notes as well.

OF TURTLES AND MICE
AND MALE RAGE

I wasn't afraid of Richard's anger when I met him. We were proud of having passionate arguments. We argued everywhere we went — his family's birthday parties, dinners with friends, dancing at the clubs. Our friends became wary of us and thought twice about the kind of night they wanted to have if Richard and I went along.

"You're not gonna fight again, are you?" they asked, rolling their eyes at each other.

"We're not fighting. We're getting to know each other. Arguing is good," Richard told them.

We argued, but I always fought back. I stood my ground, because he told me I was strong and brave and smart, and by this time I believed it. I was in graduate school. I had seen life in all its upended cacophony and survived it. I was teetering on my toes, yes, but I was still standing when the bell rang and the match was over. That is a victory.

I argued with him also because I swore not to back down when men took a position against me. I wouldn't agree with him simply because he was my boyfriend. I wouldn't vote as he did because it might mess with our relationship.

I don't remember what we argued about. Our arguments were foreplay because they didn't last long, and they didn't prevent us from dancing together, holding hands, or laughing afterward.

"Let's never go to bed angry with each other," he made me promise when I moved in with him, after a year and a half of dating. And we didn't. Not even after we had kids, well into our thirties.

I don't know exactly when I stopped arguing with him. Eventually, when he yelled, I shut down. I left the room. I went for a long walk in our neighborhood in North Carolina. I disappeared. Just like I used to do with Ann, when she was angry with me, disappointed at how I had turned out.

By the time we moved to North Carolina, our marriage was starving for nutrients we didn't know we needed to treat it back to health, to love, to mutual respect. Anger and resentment had become permanent fixtures. We tried to feed it with things: a house we couldn't have afforded in New York but could in North Carolina; private schools for our kids; date nights that required a sitter and alcohol for the expected sex; a lot of parties at our home with new friends we'd made through his job and through our kids' school friends.

Richard drank a lot at these parties, which embarrassed me because I didn't drink, and because he got loud, giving way to the New York attitude that exuded pride and grit with each word that came out of his mouth. I grew irritated, he returned the favor, and we often spent our nights listening to the other toss and turn, agitation sweating from our pores and sticking to the silk sheets scrunched between us for safe non-touching distance. I constructed these lines, made by sheets or pillows or the T-shirts he took off and tossed onto the bed when it got too hot for him.

Somewhere between there and his losing his job and telling me he wanted a divorce, the fissure became so deep, so wide, that it emerged as a ravine we didn't have the means to cross. We needed a bridge, but neither of us was skilled in constructing one, a solid one that would bring us back to each other. We made one with sticks and stones and idle hopes. It wasn't sturdy or realistic, and our resentments became even more palpable.

His bursts of rage returned me to my childhood and the mother who had grown me in violence. In my meager memories of my birth mother, Athanasia was a fury, her black hair tangled, dangling like wild weeds about her weathered and menacing features. I remember often curling into my body for shelter from her attacks, but it betrayed me with its trembling.

It betrays me still when I am fearful, when Richard's own rages unfurl like sharp daggers aimed at my chest when he is driving, at the dinner table, in the kitchen, in the bedroom, the kids always present, his voice loud and hungry for vengeance, to put me in my place, to shut me up, to bend my will, and perhaps even to take on the powerlessness and fears he felt but could not articulate without anger coiling around the wounds of his own childhood.

I sat or stood or lay beside him, my eyes closed, my heart banging against the walls of my chest, waiting like a child for relief, for silence, for love, for the rages to cease. I believed that if I stayed silent, if I did not argue back, his anger would fade, and he would give me back the tender boy who had once fostered love in me.

But that boy was gone, and all I had left of him were the two slender figures of my children that resemble him, sitting in their rooms or in the back of the car, witnessing the force and violence that words can have, the wounds they open up and leave untended, all of us left unhinged and trembling with agitation at the type of aggression that exists without fists.

But he never hit me. He knew where to draw the line. Where I would draw the line, perhaps.

And I obeyed, cowered, and surrendered, as I did in my childhood with Athanasia's physical violence and Ann's emotional debasement. They modeled who I was supposed to be in the face of stronger, more aggressive, narcissistic personalities: timid, forgiving, compliant.

They groomed me for Richard, for someone like him, who showed me kindness and love and patience and then revealed all the darkness that lay beneath, disarming me, gaslighting me for the duration of our marriage.

I didn't know how to leave him.

After all, he never hit me.

And the rest of it—the verbal assaults, the mood swings, the rages—they came and went, as erratic as his personality. Although apologies never followed them, his whistling did. His kindness came rolling back into the spaces we shared with our children, the home we built out of nothing.

I learned to push aside his volatility and anger as if they were dust particles atop our furniture, neglected and forgotten. I was used to it. Avoiding, looking the other way, polishing at the debris of destructive behavior until the surface was clean and lemon-scented. I was good at forgiving, embracing the good while dismissing the traumatic. I was touch-starved, love-starved and held onto the moments of happiness I found with Richard whenever he showed them to me. Too starved for the stability I never knew. Too emaciated for love, in any form, to walk away from it because the man I loved behaved badly a few times a week.

And he never hit me.

And my love was unconditional. I loved my father even though he left me and told me I was not his child. I loved Ann even though she dismissed and belittled me for decades. And I loved Richard, even on the days his eyes grazed over me with contempt. I love him still, today, when I look into his green eyes and recall only the good days.

But unconditional love should not exist. I have learned that it is not good for us humans —at least the ones who grew up in toxic homes and family units. Unconditional love is the kind of love hungry children need and want and fight for because they have never known it or been comforted, sheltered by it. Unconditional love is not safe because it encourages blind love, loyal love that demands you ignore its toxicity, its dysfunction, its volatility. The kind of love I searched for because my mothers taught me that I didn't deserve anything better. Anything healthier.

In Richard, I found the love that I was used to. A love familiar to that which I encountered with my mothers, forever stranded in the middle of oceanic waters without a floating device, treading water and holding my breath while the incessant force of tidal waves crashed over my head. I could only dog paddle until the storm ceased its attack. It took me a long time to realize my strength, to swim against the current, to find my voice. To know that I was too good for this numbing life, too good for people who said they loved me while peeling off pieces of my strength and kindness until there was nothing left but a beggarly, cowardly victim that reminded me much of the crumbled bones of my father.

"You teach people how to treat you," Richard often reminded me when I complained to him about people at work who spoke to me the way I would never speak to them. Friends who sprinkled passive aggressive insults into our conversations over coffee. If that is true, that I teach people how to treat me, then did I teach Ann to neglect me? And did I teach him to bark at me until I cowered and did his bidding?

His statement put the blame on me and not on them. It was my fault he no longer loved me. It was my fault that both he and Ann found me an easy target to maul with words because I didn't have their lust for winning, for conflict, for superiority over others—those with weaker personalities.

My fault, perhaps, was that I didn't set boundaries. But no one taught me I needed to set them. I didn't know I had to set them for the people I loved. For those who claimed to love me.

Because I don't impose myself on others, I suppose I don't expect people to impose themselves on me.

I am learning, the hard way, that boundaries are necessary in all relationships—with my colleagues, my children, my mother, my friends, and Richard. But they are the most difficult for me to construct. They are weak and poorly designed, but I need them for my self-preservation.

I am still unsure how I taught my adoptive mother to dislike me, but maybe I did teach Richard to disrespect me—because I stayed long after I should have—I forgave him without holding him accountable when he yelled at me, and I looked the other way instead of leaving someone who reviled me.

"Whenever he's driving and someone cuts him off, he gets so angry. He presses hard on the gas, reeling after them," I told our marriage counselor when we were still in therapy. "The kids are in the car, too, and the more I tell him to stop, the angrier he gets, the faster he drives. And when he yells at me in the car, I feel like the next thing to come at me will be his fists."

"That's understandable," Sherry said, letting her glance rest over us one at a time, like a loving mother. "Where you came from, violence was where it all led to. Your mother beat your father. Kristos hit your mother. It makes sense that you would fear that."

"I would never hit you. I never have," Richard defended himself.

"I know that. But it doesn't mean that I don't think about you hitting me. The fact that I think it's a possibility and that I shrink when you get angry at me is not normal."

Our fights have all melted into one pot of indistinguishable vegetable stew cooked for too long, something I often do because I don't cook with care. I look the other way when things get hard, as I have done in this marriage. I clamp my mouth shut; I give in; I give up. Silent and strong to the end. I endure. I tread water. What is the alternative?

Once, I wanted to buy a power washer so I could clean the grime and mold off the deck to repaint it. Richard was against it, raising his voice to a bark and insisting that I was wasting money on something I wouldn't use again. Instead of backing down, like I usually did, I went to Home Depot and bought the cheapest one I could find. My drive home was riddled with anxiety, and I constructed rebuttals to toss his way for the arguments I assumed he would rail against me. When I returned home with it and he found me taking it out of the box in the garage, he threw me a look of appreciation.

"I gotta hand it to you," he said. "I didn't think you were going to buy it."

I thought for a while, trying to fit together the puzzle of his look and the calmness in his voice. I was sure that as soon as he saw the power washer, he was going to bash into me with insults that I would collect with my trembling hands and place in a container, already flexed and fat with all the resentments I'd hidden there. But he didn't say what I expected. He didn't even yell at me.

"Because you made such a big deal out of it, you mean?" I asked for clarification.

"Yeah, you know. If you bark loud enough, people usually do what you want them to do."

"You mean, you yell at me because you know I will be afraid and not do what you don't want me to do?" I couldn't hide the incredulity hissing along the fine lines of my voice.

"Not afraid. But you know, when I bark, you back down."

I didn't respond to that. I remember going quiet suddenly, still. The psychological term for it is fog.

I thought of the time he screamed at the vet, our dog and our daughter hunched on the bench side-by-side, listening to the two men towering over them go back and forth over medicine prescribed for the dog's earache. Richard was right, the vet was wrong, and nothing else mattered—not our daughter and not the dog—not the fact that the vet had a degree and authority to back him up. Eventually, the vet backed down and gave in to Richard.

He was too strong. Too angry.

My daughter told me this story, rolling her eyes and recalling how embarrassed she was to watch her father yelling at another person. Richard chuckles when she retells it. I wonder if she was scared, and if her heart pounded against the walls of her chest.

There was the morning he chased a woman for twenty minutes because she cut him off with her car, only to realize he chased her all the way from our home to our kids' school, where she stopped her car, let her kids out in carpool, and called her husband to meet her there and confront Richard. That's how much he scared this poor woman. I don't even know how our kids felt that morning; they were in the car the entire time.

I thought of the time he yelled at our son's preschool teacher when he went to pick up Joseph's school work with the promise that our son would not be returning to a school that was okay with crossing out students' writing. He yelled at her in front of a group of small children; the teacher, terrified, asked him to leave and notified the police. The police called him afterward, ordering him to stay away from the school.

"That won't be a problem," he said, laughing, finding humor in his aggressive display.

There was the incident, a few years ago, when he chased our daughter's soccer coach on foot from the parking lot all the way across the soccer field and cursed him out for telling our daughter to hurry—she was late for the game. All this took place in front of our daughter and her teammates. The coach no longer says her name or addresses her when she plays unless it's to give her a compliment.

I remember the time, a few years ago, on our way home from Anna's, a New York-owned pizzeria in Apex, when I commented that I was overwhelmed between work and taking care of the kids while he lived and worked in New York, driving to be with us in North Carolina on the weekends. After two years of unemployment, a trading job in New York was the only position he could secure. The first year, he stayed with my mom in Queens and came home once a month, then every three weeks, and finally every weekend. For the next two years, he rented an apartment on Staten Island, but it left me doing it all alone, like a single mother.

I was driving the kids to two different schools, going to work, picking them up after school, dropping them off each day at their extra-curricular activities—piano, soccer, Tae Kwon Do, Science Olympiad, dance and social gatherings with their friends—then dinner, showers if they were willing, and bed. By the time I started on my doctoral homework and grading or planning for the courses I taught, it was after eleven at night. I had no breaks.

To make things worse, Joseph began driving to school, and the car that he used often left him stranded on highways and roadways with flat tires. Every morning was a catastrophe in trying to figure out how to get him and his sister to two different schools and me to work on time; and what to do with an anxious teenager who had just gotten his driver's license and had to navigate college searches and applications, AP exams, depression, and not knowing if he would make it to school on time because of his unreliable car.

What made all of this more difficult was parenting alone, especially after it occurred to me that Joseph was sneaking out of the house in the middle of the night to meet boys he found online. I couldn't sleep at night, and every sound in the house echoed with my son's dangerous choices. It wasn't until the pandemic struck that I was able to breathe again, sleep again, for it forced Richard back home to help me with the parenting and kept Joseph isolated in the safety of our house.

"You're never here," I told him while driving home from Anna's Pizzeria. "I do everything by myself. I'm exhausted."

But Richard didn't want to hear about my problems with doing it all, just like he didn't want to deal with them when the kids were little, and I struggled with raising them alone.

"What the fuck do you think I do?" he began. "You think this is easy for me, being away from my family? I do this for the family. I am sacrificing for my family."

"You chose to work in New York. And I'm not saying you're not sacrificing for us," I clarified. "I'm only stating that I do all of it when you're not here. And it's not like you're making money in New York. In fact, you're wasting money on gas and the apartment on Staten Island. I get no breaks, and you get to go to your apartment every night and drink wine."

"I'm a good father," he said. "I sacrifice for my kids. They mean the world to me."

"I know you do. You are a great father. When you're here. On the weekends."

And then he blew up like a dormant explosive buried beneath the sand at the bottom of the ocean. It was an explosion like no other, a hailstorm of words and low grunting vocalizations that shook through me, finding places inside my body that had remained untouched, scraping them open and gutting them.

"Stop yelling at me," I said as quietly as I could. "The kids are in the back."

But he continued, unfazed by the reminder that they sat behind us, listening, taking it all in. His anger. My reaction. I reminded him a few times of our surroundings, our kids, pleading with him to quit it, and when he didn't, I remembered his old tactic: yelling to shut me down, to ensure that I would never again mention him not being present, not comparing his absences to all the work I did without help when he wasn't around. That his sacrifice was greater than mine.

And it worked. Because I didn't bring it up again.

I made a wall out of my body, despite its need to crumble, to shrink from his attacks. I took deep breaths, slowed down my racing heartbeat, pinned my knees together for comfort, for control, and I turned all my insides into solid sheets of steel that the force of his tirade could not rip apart or penetrate. Or maybe it was my body that did this for me while Richard's rage lasted the ten minutes it took to arrive at our home, a home that I used to love to look at and found refuge in. But on that evening, Richard stormed into it.

"You're not going to divorce Dad, are you?" I remember the force of my daughter's words pulling me out of my fog long enough to settle on her round face, the golden tints in her brown eyes, and shaking my head. Satisfied, she made her way into the house.

I remained in the car alone, taking deep breaths as I concentrated on wading out of the thick fog in my brain and into the present. It was like forcing myself to drive inside the lines on a windy road set against the edge of a mountain without guard rails. I needed that level of concentration. That level of fixation, my eyes blinking hard to keep me awake, to keep me on guard.

When I got out, Joseph was there, waiting for me.

"Are you okay?" he asked.

"Yeah, I'm good. I just needed a minute."

"I love you," he said, his voice quiet, his hazel eyes, Richard's eyes, clinging to me.

"I love you, too," I told him, forcing a smile on my lips, half-bitten during the car ride. And then we walked into the house together, as if nothing had happened.

Although there were more fights, more arguments, and more submissions, his final tirade occurred during the pandemic. I hesitate to go into all the details, because this is not only my story to tell. It belongs to all of us, and our experiences of it are as different as we are. I also don't want to define it for them, my kids or Richard. Or cement it in such a light that my kids and

Richard cannot ever grow out of it, heal from it. But it is pivotal to my story, the way it hearkens back to the first memory I hold of violence, to the story of my silencing and how I learned to use the voice I was given but tucked away into the small pockets of my jeans because it was rendered irrelevant.

I can only say that it was the last straw that sliced our already fragile marriage in half, the way lightning struck our beautiful Bradford pear tree and split it into two disconnected sections a few years earlier.

Joseph used to climb that tree when he was little. I have pictures of him, wearing his red Gap sweatshirt and jeans, his almost black hair disheveled, loose strands slipping into his eyes, smiling as he stood upon a thick branch deep into the tree. He made a nest out of it, and he and his neighborhood friends climbed into it and called it their clubhouse.

I used to look forward to driving home after picking up the kids from school in the springtime, and I slowed down the car, moved closer to my front window, the wheel pressed against my chest, just to capture—in slow motion—the sight of the white flowers blossoming from the tree for a week or two before wilting and falling to the ground, making a bed of snowy petals a gust of wind eventually cleared away. I loved that tree, more than the magnolias on the side of our house or the cherry trees whose pink petals needed to be scooped off the surface of our in-ground pool every spring when they bloomed and inevitably wilted and fell from their homes.

When this tree split in half and was cut into pieces, put on a truck, and taken away from our front yard, it felt like foreshadowing to me. Even though a few months later, I replaced it with a cherry tree I bought from Home Depot, something was different. I felt a change. A pivotal loss.

It was the same after Richard's last violent outburst.

He expected us to have dinner in the dining room every

night, setting the table with our wedding china, serving us filet mignon, as a family. But every dinner as a family resulted in small volcanic eruptions between Joseph and Richard as Rena watched quietly from her seat, and I found myself in a state of hypervigilance, trying to pacify one male or the other, as they attempted to voice their opinions and be heard. Getting Joseph to join us for dinner was a hardship, but this night, he came downstairs and ate with us.

Everything was okay until it wasn't. Until they began arguing about Black Lives Matter, police brutality, and the protests sprinkling the cities during the pandemic. Their political views divided them, and Joseph struggled to be seen by a father who voted for the party that suppressed his son's rights as a gay man.

At one point, Joseph turned his eyes to me. "I can't talk to him." He rose from the table, took his plate to the kitchen, and placed it in the sink. Richard followed him in that quick stride he has.

I was still in the dining room, sitting down with Rena, both of us rolling our eyes at each other, wishing Richard would stop arguing, trying to prove how right he was to a seventeen-year-old. My skin tingled with trepidation, and as Rena spoke to me, my eyes were on my son, vigilant, my body wired for the conflict it recalled from my childhood.

"Shut up," Joseph told him.

Next thing I know, Richard's body moved in on Joseph's, his finger thrust in our son's face. His pink skin was already flushed, steaming with rage, his teeth gritted to show his opponent that this was only the surface of what lay beneath.

Watching from the dining room, my skin vibrated with fear as Joseph turned his back to Richard, thought twice, and then faced him, his body long and erect, his chin up, his features ready for a fight.

The two bodies collided, one tall and thin with only bones holding it together, the other shorter but thick and wide. Richard's hands grabbed Joseph's T-shirt, his breath hot against our son's face. Joseph couldn't have escaped the grip even if he'd wanted to. He was no match for his father.

That was my signal. My trigger from a long time ago when my mother attacked my father until blood poured out of him, and I sat at the kitchen table beside my brothers, afraid to scream or run or do anything other than sit and swallow the scene unfolding before me.

But I wasn't four anymore. I was a mother, and without thinking, I ran into the kitchen and inserted my body between theirs. I saw Richard's fingers with a bunch of Joseph's T-shirt material clenched inside them, circled into a fist, pushing against Joseph's neck. I had to press myself in there, but when I did, I placed one hand on Joseph's chest, the other against Richard's chest, and I pushed as hard as I could.

"Stop it! Stop it! Stop it!" I screamed at Richard, my back set against Joseph's lean frame like a shield, my hands shoving Richard's bulky form in the opposite direction—once, twice, three times. Eventually, he backed away, his skin red and puffy with rage.

"What the fuck are you doing?" I screamed. "He's your kid!"

I turned to face Joseph and caught a glimpse of Rena, still standing in the dining room, her hands clasped against her mouth, crying. The image of her, frozen with trepidation at the age of thirteen, reminds me of me at four, watching my parents fight. I wonder if this will be the memory that haunts her. That fractures the already fragile state of our family. The one that repeats itself in her adult life—as mine repeated itself in this one moment, between my husband and my son—an echo from the past.

"Joseph, please go to your room. Please," I begged him, and I felt like I could breathe again only when he finally walked out of the kitchen and disappeared up the stairs.

And then I broke down. My shoulders bent over, my arms strapped the sides of my stomach, and unbridled sobs spewed like vomit out of my mouth. I ambled toward the dining room to sit down.

Rena came up to me, put her hands on my hair, smoothed it with her long, thin fingers, and said, "It's okay, Mom. It's okay."

"None of this is okay," I let her know between gasps of air. I wouldn't normalize this behavior for her. Parents don't attack their kids, verbally or physically. It's not normal. It shouldn't be.

My kids felt a change that day, just as I had known at four, when my father ran out of our home with a stab wound in his eye, blood pouring out of him as if it were escaping a prison of his making, that nothing would ever be the same again. But they couldn't put their fingers on what exactly, other than that some veneer had been lifted, and the raw and hidden flaws of our family were finally laid open and made vulnerable. None of us could hide from it, pretend it hadn't happened.

"I want a divorce!" I yelled at Richard a few minutes later, when Joseph stole back into his room and Rena burrowed into hers, waiting out the storm. He was out in the backyard, pulling dead, limp, and wet leaves from the surface of our pool.

I stormed back into the house and found refuge on my bed — our bed — switching on the television set that I had been using these many years to numb me, to still the fear thrashing against my chest.

I had finally done it. I was ready. Ready to leave. Ready to vacate the sinkhole this marriage had become, filled with toxic interactions and unvoiced unhappiness wrapped around my legs and throat like thick vines, unwilling to let me go.

He came into our room, and without looking at me, set the conditions for our divorce.

"If we divorce," his voice splintered my thoughts, "I will fight you for Rena."

Numbness coursed through me, reaching my throat, choking me with silence and fear. I was nauseous.

"Why?" I asked when I found my voice. "Why can't we just leave each other and not put our kids through the ringer? Fighting for custody will hurt them."

"You know who you married," he reminded me.

An ache grew inside me like a weed I couldn't extract from the ashy soil of our marriage. I was reeling from making a choice over my children and their happiness: Do I leave for the sake of one child? Or stay for the sake of the other? How do I choose? How could I end all things when the spine that held me up and together was made of nothing more than rubber and glue?

But Richard knew me. He knew the threat would work on me. That fear would rule and govern my choices. If I left, my kids would suffer.

And so I stayed.

It took me another year. A year of therapy, of bravery-building. A year of lying beside him with a wide, empty space of polluted air hunched between us like an old, grouchy man to find the courage, the resolve to leave him. A year for the fear of leaving him to bleed into strength and determination.

Every night I went to bed reimagining that scene from Elizabeth Gilbert's memoir *Eat, Pray, Love*, in which she found herself on her knees in the bathroom, weeping while her husband slept in the next room, knowing she wanted to end her marriage but unable to find the words, the courage she needed to extricate herself from a marriage that made her unhappy.

And one night, at the tail end of the summer before Joseph was to leave for college and Rena would be entering high school, I shut my eyes, opened my mouth, and gave birth to the words I knew would change everything, for all of us.

"Richard," I began, my eyes still shut against the dark room, listening to his breathing beside me. "Are you happy?"

"Not particularly," he returned, his voice on edge, crisp and dry, sullen even. As if he knew what was coming.

"Then what are we doing here?"

"Just say it, Marina," was his bitter reply.

"I want to separate. Get a divorce. I don't want to do this anymore."

I don't recall what he said after that. He left the room. And I lay in bed, giddy, my heart humming with relief, with a sense of freedom I hadn't felt since the day I left my mother's home to move in with him on the summer of my twenty-fifth birthday.

Ironically, this was the summer of my fiftieth birthday. I had left the shackles of one relationship for love, and twenty-five years later, I was disentangling my limbs from the mangled roots of that same love. Not for the love of someone else. Not to be with anyone else. But for me. To save me. To free myself from a marriage and an existence that felt much like a slow and formidable death.

"I thought your mother was a turtle," Richard confessed to our son the night we told the kids we were separating. I didn't hear this, but Joseph told me. Richard confronted him when I was not around, out in the driveway, full of anger again, and Joseph, with heart pounding in his ears, stopped his father's verbal attack by asking, "Why are you doing this? I'm your son!"

"I'm used to it," he said. "I do it to your mother, and you're just like her."

"I threw knives at her," he continued in his explanation, "but I thought she was a turtle and that they would bounce off her. But she turned out to be a mouse, and every time I threw a knife at her, she didn't move, and I just kept cutting off limb after limb."

It was a strange analogy, but it showed me that Richard had known what he was doing. He didn't expect his attacks to stick, to bind me, or harm me. But they did, to the point where they paralyzed me, left me without the limbs I needed to move out of the way.

It wasn't until I recapped the conversation with my therapist that I realized the most important point about this analogy: Why throw knives at all? Why throw them at people you love? At family?

It took a long time and a lot of energy and spine-building to leave the only relationship I had ever known outside the one I had shared with my adoptive mother, but it had become a relationship that no longer operated on love and respect. Taking nothing more than my son, my daughter, our three kittens, and my books, I moved out of the big house I was no longer invested in and a marriage that made me feel small and worthless. Within a week, I had moved into a small, rundown apartment I could afford on my teacher's salary. I was broke and filled with consternation, but walking away had left me whole and sane and free — if not happy.

And happy will come. I know it, because this time, my happiness is not wrapped up in someone else or in the expectations they have for me to please them, to be the kind of person they can live with — compliant and full of surrenders that deplete my confidence and self-respect — until there is only a ghost looking back at me from the mirror, her eyes gaunt and vacant and sad.

I'm neither a turtle nor a mouse. I'm just me. Marina.

I have agency. Self-assertion. I won't sacrifice myself, won't give up parts of myself to fit anyone else's expectations until I am no longer recognizable to myself. I am learning to love myself in ways no one else has been willing to love me until now.

Without self-erasure. Without looking the other way.

HAPPY (UN)ENDING

W hat does a happy ending look like for a fifty-year-old unsexed, divorced woman who wears trauma like an oversized
sweatshirt intended to hide invisible scars and unhealed wounds?

There is no happy ending. My story is in the present, the
middle, really, where all the pieces are still knotted, albeit slightly
loose, and the burns from cigarette butts are scabbed remnants
on both wrists, the pain faded, the scars rounded and brown. A
spot that cannot be erased or excised, but is in the long and
overdue process of healing.

But there is no ending, either. This is not the end. I am still
here, holding on, grasping at things to keep me upright and pull
me forward. I carry trauma with me wherever I go, as if it's one
of those small-sized dogs celebrities tuck into their pocketbooks.
I pet it occasionally, when it shivers with fear, but mostly, it sits
among my possessions and whines until I take it home and it
feels safe again.

My fears and anxieties cost me my independence, my feminism, the core of my existence. I want to be strong enough,
confident enough to travel on my own, to parent without fear of
setting boundaries, to live on my own, to live each day without
wanting it to be my last because I am just so tired of fighting,
feeling so damn hungry all the time for things that have nothing
to do with food.

I want to meet the day when I no longer want to lie down in my school's hallway or the ground at the closest intersection, curl into a ball, and surrender, close my eyes and go to sleep. To not want to die, to not want to be put in a nursing home for the sake of waiting to die, alone and attended to by strangers who change my sheets and help me from one lonely corridor of life to the next until there are no more corridors and no more breaths left.

I want *to want* to live, to laugh for longer than one moment that only comes once in a while. I want to find joy, to swim in it, to feel it all over my body the way the sun's rays strike me with warmth, a bubble of vibrant gases imploding inside me.

Hunger continues to dance along the hairs of my arms and legs like a stubborn mosquito mistaking me for a hard, still branch, stinging me when I actually move and shock it to the core of its own need for survival. It's an annoyance I am forced to smack off me when it digs its tentacles into the thick layers of my skin, prying me open for a taste, a knowing of me that leaves me itching for relief that never comes.

It's the kind of hunger no amount of food will satisfy. I stand in front of the refrigerator with the doors open and toss grapes, olives, cherries into my mouth. I close the doors and walk away just to return a few minutes later, cutting up cheddar cheese, pairing each slice with a rounded cracker, and sending them to my stomach, like old-fashioned telegrams, warning it to cease its assault and never-ending calls for attention.

I stand in front of the pantry this time. Maybe I need sugar. I pop four vanilla wafers, one after the other, down the hatch. I sit and do some grading, some writing, some Netflix bingeing, and I need to eat something else: leftover cold filet mignon made the night before, salted and grilled to perfection. But the holes in me are deep and wide, so I fill them up with Coke and coffee, weighing myself each morning and praying I haven't gained one more pound of self-loathing I don't have the strength to carry anymore.

Sometimes, I think Greek food, the food of my childhood, battered in oil and salt and lost memories, will fill the tumorous tunnels scraping along the highways of my entrails. So I drag myself to Greek restaurants, bake pastitsio, a three-hour ordeal, or take trips to Greece to sit at wooden tables adorned with blue-and-white checkered tablecloths, Eleni and Stavros seated beside me, across from me, plates full of my childhood favorites at the center: pastitsio, tiropita, chicken nestled in pita and tzatziki sauce, spanakopita, thick fries, horiatiki salata, the authentic Greek salad. While the moment is euphoric and uplifting, making me feel complete and whole and happy, it eventually loosens like a stain doused with bleach and disappears into a blank slate of white background with no color or vibrancy in sight. Just a memory. Just a moment, lost in a cough or a sneeze.

When food is obviously not the answer, I feed myself in other ways. I write. I teach. I force my fears to sit in the audience, like a quiet student, while I lecture about books and writing and women's rights in classrooms that hold my authority at its center. I direct the honors program at my college, recruiting faculty, organizing presentations, rallying my students, guiding their honors projects, holding the title of director like a shield against my armor, a warrior who leads and mentors and thrives. I sign up for grants and conferences requiring me to present my research, and with trembling bones and clammy palms, I stare down my anxieties one at a time, telling them to go fuck themselves, to die where they sit, lodged in my throat. It's my turn to speak.

I throw myself back into school for a PhD in Education with a focus on trauma and bibliotherapy, conducting research I once believed I wasn't smart enough to delve into—like mixed methods research and quantitative analysis. I am at home in school not only as a teacher but also as a student. I don't miss deadlines or drop all the balls suspended above my head, no matter how chaotic my personal life is with talks of divorce or loss of jobs or trust or love.

School is safe—the only place that makes me feel comfortable in my skin, learning, growing, proving to myself, one degree at a time, that I am smart, I am smart, I am smart. I am a fraud hiding behind achievements and wide-toothed smiles. It's all a pretense. I don't have it all together, and I don't think I ever will.

I don't know anyone who does. The more women I meet, the more messiness I encounter. Women who want to be strong and collected and happy, who strive for these things, but who are also flailing around, like fish pulled out of water, gasping for relief, oxygen in their lungs, or a quick and easy death. Women who want nothing more than to be seen and loved.

I find comfort in my friends, realizing how unkind life has been to so many women in my circle. How strong they are. How important it is to show up for them the way they have been showing up for me. My circle of women is small and contained, but it has given me the strength to move forward, to hope, to love again.

There is comfort in my kids. Joseph entrusts me with his secrets, his sex-capades, the drugs he's experimenting with at school, and we talk about suicide, divorce, love, and the importance of mental health for both of us. He entrusts me with his heart, as much of it as he is willing to share. He entrusts me with his friends, telling me about this one who is depressed, this one who is a racist, this one who tried to kill herself, the one who did kill himself.

I want to swaddle him the way he was brought to me after I gave birth to him, tightly bound in a blue blanket and placed in my arms for safety and protection, for the love of him pouring out of my pores and swimming in my eyes every time I inhale the sight of his long, lanky, still boyish-looking frame, the dark, stringy strands of hair that fall into his eyes, those hazel eyes that always seem so tender and open when they look at me.

I take comfort in knowing that when he goes out on his own, he will do so with the confidence that he is loved. That he will always have a home, a tribe to fall back into or return to when he needs it the most. I will always worry about him, about the anger hanging on his upturned chin when he knows he is being watched and refuses to engage the pair of eyes waiting to be invited in. My eyes, taking him in like scoops of sugar I load into my coffee each morning.

I wonder if the back of my knees will always shudder when I fear for him as they do whenever he cuts himself and his blood gushes out, or he gets a severe sunburn because I took him to the beach and didn't make him apply sun protection to his pale, white skin on an overcast day. Seven miserable and painful days ensued, and I bit my nails every time he came into the kitchen for a snack, his long limbs feverish and red, stiffly carrying him up and down the stairs, in and out of my line of vision.

I pray his anxieties and self-isolation are part of the normal teenage angst and not related to memories he has of me raising him as a toddler, when I was all but a toddler myself, dressing up like an adult, pretending to assume roles of motherhood I never experienced before, and of all the mistakes I made in raising him with the desperation of an inexperienced mom.

I take comfort in the way he reads me without words, sensing my awkwardness around deep conversations and my interminable displays of physical affection toward my children. He hugs me back when I hug him. He kisses me back when I kiss him. And he says, "I love you, too," each time I say the words to him.

I try to fill his pockets with all the love I hold for him, as much as he lets me, and I hope this is enough. That I have not failed in some unmistakable and unforeseen way that will debilitate him from making connections and forging tribes to treasure and love him as I do.

I find comfort in my daughter, now fifteen, and the three

years remaining before she goes off to her own life and college. Rena is still in the sweet spot of adolescence that requires hugs and kisses before she goes to sleep, her arms wrapped around the soft cat she has claimed as her own, as if she were holding a baby, the way I once held her to my chest, her mouth and cheek rubbing against the thick, matted hairs of an animal she's known since her infancy.

Rena is torn between love and anger toward me, and I often find her looking at me the way I used to look at my own adoptive mother, the way I used to dismiss her with a roll of the eyes, a wave of the wrist.

I fractured her security when I left her father, and there is a growing anger in her toward me that a people pleaser like me finds difficult to endure. I hold her lightly, letting her decide who she wants to stay with and when, and I walk on eggshells around her, because if I tug at her too much and for too long, I know I will lose her for good.

I don't always know how to engage her, how to appease her, so I do what my mothers didn't do. I force her into hugs, pulling her arms away from her chest where they hang limply for a few seconds and then reciprocate, clinging to the skin on my back. I bandage her wounds when she tears her knees and cradle her when she stubs a toe or cracks an elbow against hard door frames she doesn't see because she never looks forward, her head always cocked over her shoulder, behind her. I tell her I love her multiple times a day, so she hears the words and feels the full, inimitable love living in me for her.

But I am dismissive, too. I laugh at the wrong things. I cut her off. I lack the patience to hear all the details of her day. Her needs force me to communicate, to talk, to reveal myself in ways that go against my nature. She unearths my voice and teaches me how important it is to use that voice. Her voice is strong, loud, open, emotional, and upfront, and each time she uses it, I know that, despite my flaws, I did something right as her mother. I never stifled her voice, diminishing her power. When I release her out into the world, I know she will be better than me, stronger, wiser, with the kind of organic agency and power I have struggled to form in myself.

I find comfort in my body, the one that sags now, the loose skin on my stomach and rib cage, the belly protruding slightly, the nerve endings still numb from my hysterectomy, the scar line running along the top of my pubic bone, almost hidden. I don't feel less of a woman because I am missing a uterus. I have never defined my womanhood by the way my body looks, by the size of my breasts, or the fact I used to be super-fertile, as my IVF nurses used to tell me, wondering why it was so hard for me to get pregnant.

"I think you don't have enough sex," one of my male doctors once told me with a wink. "Go home and have sex with your husband. You'll get pregnant before you know it."

But sex was never something that made me comfortable. It was a thinly threaded blanket placed over me that never made me feel quite warm enough, secure enough. I did it because I had to. I was married. It's what married people do. So I take comfort in not having sex. In getting to know my body and my needs outside of male desires, male expectations that have always used me and my body as expendable receptacles of men's wishes and frustrations.

"You need a real man," my oldest friend said to me over the phone. She divorced her husband of twenty-five years because she wanted love, the romantic, head-over-heels love her marriage had never been about.

"Maybe you need a woman," my newest friend recently told me, steeped in her newfound understanding of tarot cards and astrological signs. She revealed to me that in my past life I was a high priestess, and it makes sense to her that I have searched for love in the wrong sex.

"I'm not attracted to women." I shook my head at her, laughing. "I love women, but not in that way."

The truth is, I have spent my entire life seeking love in others. In my mothers. My father. In men. In Richard. But they have all abandoned me, sacrificed me as they sought to feed their own love-hungers.

Like many parents, I also expected to find love through my children, often feeling empty when they didn't express it the way I needed them to. With them, it's clearer, though. I am not here to gain their love. Their love for me is not at the precipice—nor should it be—of my existence. Or theirs.

I need to love them so hard and so deep that they feel it and never have to question it. I must put them out into the world so loved that they don't search endlessly for it just to land in the empty baskets of the wrong love mates—those who have nothing to offer them but more emptiness. If I do my job right, grow them secure with love and openness, then they will not hunger as I have, settling for the first unworthy bits of nurturance they find, feeding themselves without ever feeling full or satiated because they have found love in the wrong places and in the wrong people. I must teach them to love themselves first and to value that love over the love of anyone else. People come and go, but we're stuck with the bodies we were born to and grow up fitting into.

I don't need a man—or a woman—to love me or to make me feel whole. No other human should have this kind of power over me—over another human. We should all be going into the world full and satisfied with ourselves, seeking only kinship, friendship, companionship in one another. But not the answers to our existence.

Love cannot be found out there, in the arms of people who have their own demons to expel and hungers to feed. The best kind of love can only be found at home. In the home we carry with us wherever we go. When we are at home with our body, we have found love. The kind of love that cannot be replaced or ever taken away from us. Self-love. When we look for it in others, we will always come home empty. We will always feel lacking and unfulfilled. This has been my life. My lesson.

I look at my body in the mornings now, before I hop in the shower, and I don't feel shame in looking at it. I don't have a flat belly. It's rounded in the middle, and when I bend over, there are three rolls of loose skin bunching up in waves. My breasts have never been large and fall in the small range, but I have always been content with them.

This is my body. Short with thick legs that remind me how strong I am, how present my body is in this world that often renders me invisible because it is a female body—an aging body. My skin is soft and elastic, no longer riddled with acne but with age spots sprouting like flowers all over me.

This is my body. A fifty-year-old's body, and for the first time in my life, I have control of it. What happens to it. How I move in it. How I dress it. How it serves me. I don't have to share it, unless I want to. My body is the home my kids can return to for solace and a reminder of their childhood, their innocence, where they can still be loved for being themselves, no matter the choices they have made or want to make.

I have learned to care for my body, listen to it instead of pretending it is not attached to me. I slow down when it asks for a pause in time. I feed it when it is hungry. Hydrate it with water instead of bearing it down with caffeine and sugar. I nurture it as if it were one of my children.

I take myself for walks at night, the way my father and I used to walk together in Greece when I was a little girl. I return to him on those walks, a lone shadow strolling along the dark streets, pretending he is walking beside me, looking as he did when I was seven, bowed and crumpled, his long face gaunt and lost in thought, his eyes haunted by a life he escaped.

I think of him a lot, wishing I had known more about him, recalled more of him than the few memories I do possess of him being abused and deserting me. I pretend he is with me on my daily ten-thousand-step walks, and every time I pass blue flickering lights of television sets flashing through the filter of curtains on a windowpane, a smile stretches across my thin lips, wan and homesick, but still, a smile that is grateful for this one good memory that always brings me back to my father.

I spent my adult years with a man who was unlike my father because I made myself believe that my father's gentleness and softness were weaknesses. He had been abused because he was weak. He left because he was weak. But that belief only drew me into the arms of a man who was good until he wasn't. Until only the aggressive, angry, and explosive parts showed themselves. A man more like the Kristos of my childhood, a man I feared and loathed, than the father who should have modeled men for me.

So determined was I to find a man unlike my father, resentful of him for abandoning his kids for the sake of his own survival, that I found the one man in the universe who possessed Kristos's volatility, Athanasia's rages, and Ann's denials of me. All three were narcissists, and the codependent empath in me sought them out because this is all I knew. All I understood.

Cognizant now of steering away from narcissists, and how easy it is for me to find them, to align my life to theirs, I navigate dating with eyes open, my senses sharp and wired for red flags my therapist, Laura, processes with me during our sessions. Dating was part of my therapy work because Laura wanted me to find love, to give voice to the love and vibrancy that lives in me still, despite it all. The pain, the losses, the disappointments, the fears.

"Don't let them win," she told me. "Don't shut yourself down. You deserve to be happy. To be loved. To love."

And then I met Simon. A man who reminds me of my father.

The gentle, loving, kind parts of him that call out to me from my childhood.

He came into my life like a soft, vibrant light peeking through the dark curtains I had drawn over my heart and body, enclosing me in corners of self-denials. In the early hours of the day, he is there, gently prodding away the debris and dark elements, awakening the sleepy and anesthetized parts of my heart and sexuality.

And I let him. I let him slip into me like an antidote to my unsexedness. My body craves him, his touch, his lips on my mouth. I listen to her and give her what she wants. I have denied her long enough. Denied myself long enough.

For the first time since I was twenty-three and settled down with Richard, I find a sexy, wanting woman in me. One who thrills at the possibility of there being more to life than aching pangs of emptiness.

Simon has been the only man since my early years with Richard who has come to me unexpectedly when I had all but given up on love and sex or connecting with another member of the opposite sex. But here I am, questioning myself, reassessing my body's desires, reveling in butterflies and racing heartbeats that I believed I would never know again. And I wonder if there is more out there for me. For all of us seeking the courage to move out of unlovedness, unsexedness.

I am older this time around, more confident, surprised that the years I have endured as an unsexed woman had more to do with trauma and lack of emotional safety than with my own sexual desires—that apparently exist—breathing quietly beneath the surface of skin that has not been touched with love, out of love, out of desire for over a decade.

There is still love and desire in these old bones. In this old body. In this hurting shell of a woman who continues to rise, to adapt, to hunger for so much more than the nothingness I was once willing to accept as part of my life, waiting it out until my last dying breath — in misery, in loneliness.

I look at my reflection in the mirror now, and I see a lovely, smiling, laughing woman looking back at me. I find hope in my eyes, sex in my thoughts, and song in my lungs.

I am strong. I am smart. I am beautiful.

I am even pretty damn sexy when I want to be. When I am free to love and be loved on my own terms.

And I am sexed.

Not over. Not under. Not unsexed.

But beautifully, incandescently sexed.

ABOUT THE AUTHOR

Marina DelVecchio, PhD, is a college professor and writer. In addition to her online publications in MS Magazine, Huffington Post, and The New Agenda, her book publications include *Dear Jane, The Professor's Wife*, and *The Virgin Chronicles*. She teaches women's studies and literature through the lens of bibliotherapy, guiding her students to connect with literary heroes who write for power and self-assertion. She lives in North Carolina with her children and three feral cats.

SELECTED TITLES FROM SHE WRITES PRESS

She Writes Press is an independent publishing company founded to serve women writers everywhere. Visit us at www.shewritespress.com.

The Virgin Chronicles: A Memoir by Marina DelVecchio. $16.95, 978-1-64742-337-7. Marina DelVecchio's biological mother was a prostitute who taught her to fear sex. Her adoptive mother was a virgin who taught her that sex was shameful and dirty. Stuck between these two polarizing mothers and their dysfunctions, Marina struggles to find not only her own sexual power but also her own voice.

Promenade of Desire: A Barcelona Memoir by Isidra Mencos. $17.95, 978-1-64742-251-6. *Promenade of Desire* narrates a young woman's journey from repression to liberation in tandem with Spain's transition from dictatorship to democracy. As the country transforms itself, the shy María Isidra evolves into the alluring Isadora, whose passion for books and salsa dancing sustains her as she discovers what it means to be lustful and loved, and succeeds in reclaiming her whole self.

The Strongbox: Searching for My Absent Father by Terry Sue Harms. $16.95, 978-1-63152-775-3. Following the unexpected death of her alcoholic mother, sixteen-year-old Terry Sue decides her biological father, whom she doesn't know, could change her life for the better. By the time she finally finds him, however—after decades of searching—she understands that she has cultivated the nurturing she craved from him for herself.

The Space Between: A Memoir of Mother-Daughter Love at the End of Life by Virginia A. Simpson. $16.95, 978-1-63152-049-5. When a life-threatening illness makes it necessary for Virginia Simpson's mother, Ruth, to come live with her, Simpson struggles to heal their relationship before Ruth dies.

The S Word by Paolina Milana. $16.95, 978-1-63152-927-6. An insider's account of growing up with a schizophrenic mother, and the disastrous toll the illness—and her Sicilian Catholic family's code of secrecy—takes upon her young life.

Printed in the USA
CPSIA information can be obtained
at www.ICGtesting.com
JSHW082255200624
65153JS00001B/1

9 781647 426941